Who is this King?

To Ellie

One step at a time
with Jesus takes
you to glory

Love + blessings
Rose

Who is this King?

Rose George

RoperPenberthy Publishing Ltd
Horsham, England

Published by RoperPenberthy Publishing Ltd
PO Box 545, Horsham, England

All Bible quotations are from the New International Version,
unless otherwise stated

First published in 2003

ISBN 1 903905 12 5

Cover design by Angie Moyler

Typeset by Avocet Typeset, Chilton, Aylesbury, Bucks
Printed in the United Kingdom by Cox & Wyman Ltd, Reading, Berks

Dedication

This book is dedicated to my daughter Keeli
and my husband Gerry.

Keeli, for many years you were my reason for living, then I
gave you back to Jesus and He released us both into the plan
He had for each of us. My prayer for you is that you will
always keep a passion for Jesus at the centre of that plan –
a prayer that I know has already been answered.

Gerry, thank you for believing in me and encouraging me to
start writing even when I didn't think I knew how, and for
sharing me with the computer for so long! You never
complained, even when I was so engrossed that I forgot the
mealtimes.

I love you both.

Rose and Mum.

Acknowledgements

My Jesus, my wonderful Lord who by His grace chose to
write this book through me. You are a God of the
impossible. Thank you that you are more than willing and

able to do immeasurably more than all I could ask or imagine, according to your power at work within me.

My husband Gerry, for believing in me and encouraging me to start writing even when I didn't think I knew how, and for sharing me with the computer for so long. You never complained, even when I was so engrossed that I forgot the mealtimes.

Susie – thank you for your hard work in sorting out spelling and punctuation, and for your obedience when the Lord told you to offer to help.

Norma – your prayer support and encouragement throughout was invaluable, thanks also for writing the bit: 'About the Author'.

Melanie – for being just as excited as I was about producing the cover photograph. When I described what I had seen in the Spirit, you saw it too. Praise God! Sean and Stephanie - for giving a whole day for the photo shoot and being such great models.

Thanks also for Bridget for looking after us so well that day, and for the loan of your wedding dress and wonderful garden for the shoot.

And lastly, I thank all the many people too numerous to mention, who encouraged, believed and prayed for me. I really appreciate you all. Thank you.

Rose George, October 2003

Contents

Foreword

This book can be a great help to you. It combines clear teaching from God's Word with personal testimony that will draw you into a closer encounter and relationship with Jesus Christ. Rose George's writing is full of the experience of God's love and will show you how that love can become more real for you personally.

'Who is this King?' keeps close to the words of scripture showing you how to experience the spiritual freedom Christ died to make possible for you. Yet this is a book that will also encourage you to look out beyond yourself and your own needs, and see how God can use you to make His love known to others.

Rose George helps you to understand what it means to be a truly holy person, not someone locked up in pious religious attitudes, but called and set apart by the Lord for His purposes. She shows how such holiness is God's will for all His children and is therefore readily available for every believer through His grace.

I applaud Rose's clear, simple yet profound way of teaching the truth. Like her you can have a heart after God, an enduring love for Him and a vision of His win and purpose for your life that He will enable you to fulfill.

Colin Urquhart

Introduction

"Lord, I want to live, eat, sleep and breathe Your Word." This was the cry of my heart when I first received Jesus as my personal Saviour. I had tried religion and didn't want it, for it was boring and impersonal. This was a personal *relationship* with a *real* person, someone who was *alive* and who cared about *me,* and I wanted to get to know Him. I wanted to 'live, eat, sleep and breathe' Jesus. I had an inheritance in Him and I wanted to know what it was. Reading, retaining, and understanding the Bible was something I didn't find easy, and I was such a slow reader that by the time I reached the end of a chapter, I had forgotten the beginning. So I praise God that when He chose me, He knew what He was getting. He chose me before the beginning of time and He wasn't surprised at what He was getting. He didn't have to adjust His plan to accommodate my shortcomings. He chose me especially for the plan He has for me, which is to be like Him. He chooses the weak and foolish things of this world to shame the wise and to show His glory. Recently I said to the Lord, "Show me how to worship You in Spirit and truth, to *really* worship You in Spirit and truth." And His answer was, "It's not an experience, Rose, it's a lifestyle." God wants your whole life to be a love song to Him.

'*In his great mercy he has given us new birth into a living hope through the resurrection of Jesus Christ from the dead, and into an inheritance that can never perish, spoil or fade – kept in heaven for you.*' 1 Peter 1:3–4.

We are on a journey with Jesus to our inheritance in Heaven.

> *'For he chose us in him before the creation of the world to be holy and blameless in his sight. In love he predestined us to be adopted as his sons through Jesus Christ ... '* Eph. 1:4–5.

If He chose us even before creation to be set apart for Him and to be blameless, washed clean and forgiven, if He planned it way back then for us to be His sons, then surely that means that He also knew that it would be possible. He is a God of variety who created us all to be unique, and so 'in love', He will teach us in a way that we can understand how to walk this walk and live this set apart life with Him.Psalm 119: 1–2 says, *'Blessed are they whose ways are blameless, who walk according to the law of the LORD. Blessed are they who keep his statutes and seek him with all their heart.'* We were chosen to be blameless through Jesus, but the key is for us to seek Him with all our heart and then He will enable us to walk in His ways and so receive the blessings of God. My prayer for this book is that it will encourage ordinary people like myself and draw them into a deeper and more intimate relationship with Jesus and a greater revelation of the Father in some of the ways that He has used to teach me, such as dreams, visions, revelations, testimonies and personal experiences. I also pray that all who read it will come with open minds to the things of God, with teachable spirits and hearts desiring to really *know* – who is this King? No-one is ready to go deeper unless they are dissatisfied with where they are.

1

Chosen For A Purpose

Many years ago, in a town called Nazareth in Galilee, a baby girl was born. All we know about her is that her parents were from the priestly tribe of the Jews, descendants of Aaron, and that she had relatives in Judea called Elizabeth and Zechariah. No-one knew the destiny that was in store for this child. She was just another Jewish baby … but God had a plan for her life that would change the world forever. As was the custom with Jewish families, Mary, as the child was called, grew up hearing the many stories passed down from generation to generation about God and the prophets of old. How God had brought the Jewish people out of Egypt, about Adam and Eve, the first man and woman, who were thrown out of the garden of Eden because they disobeyed God, about Abraham, Moses, Elijah and Elisha, Ezekiel and many others who spoke of a promised Messiah, a Saviour. Stories that she loved to hear, not realising that soon she was to be confronted with whether she really believed what she had heard and learned. When Mary was about fifteen years old, still a virgin and pledged to be married to a man called Joseph, a descendant of David, she was visited by an angel who said to her, "Greetings, you who are highly favoured! The Lord is with you." She was terrified, for she'd never seen an angel before. What could he want with her? But the angel said to Mary, "Don't be afraid. God has decided to bless you! Very soon now, you will become pregnant and you will give birth to a son, whom you are to name 'Jesus'. He will be very great and will be called the Son of God. And the Lord God will give Him the throne of His ancestor David. He's going to reign over Israel forever, a never ending kingdom!"Mary's thoughts were spinning, for surely this angel was talking about the promised Messiah. Could this really be possible, that *she* was to become the mother of the Son of God? "But how can this be?" she asked out loud. "How can I have a baby? I'm a virgin." The angel replied, "The Holy Spirit will come upon you, and the power of the Most High will overshadow you. So the baby born to you will be very holy, and He will be called the Son of God. And what's more, your relative Elizabeth, whom everyone thought barren, is also going to have a baby and is already in her sixth month. You see, nothing is impossible with God."

Wow! It all seemed crazy, like a crazy dream, a nightmare … and yet … something stirred in her heart … Mary knew she had a decision to make. Was she *really* willing to give everything she had to obey the God whom she professed to serve? To give up any plans she had of her own and risk rejection from Joseph and from her family? The Jewish Law said that she could be stoned to death. Was she prepared for that? Somehow, against all natural sense, she *knew* that the God whom she served was bigger than all these things. Nothing made sense from the human perspective and yet … somehow she believed! She was faced with the truth of God's word and responded, "I am the Lord's servant and am willing to accept whatever He wants. May it be to me as you have said."

Have you ever really thought what an awesome decision that was for Mary to make? It comes from a passage in the Bible, from the first chapter of Luke, that we all know so well, and sometimes I think we make light of it. This young

Jewish girl named Mary was visited by an angel, who told her that she was going to have a baby. She was to call Him Jesus and He would be the Son of God. Although she was 'greatly troubled' by the news and asked how it could be, as soon as the angel said that the Holy Spirit would do it, Mary simply consented and she was fine. It all sounds so easy. That was certainly how I had read it. Oh, I loved the story and I always saw Mary as a wonderful role model for submission to God. Even part of my own call as a Christian came from this story. But recently I have started to see Mary as far more real than I had ever seen her before. I can relate to her now because I can see that she was just like me – ordinary.

I have been a Christian for a number of years and have been married to Gerry for the last five of those years. (I got more than I bargained for when I went to Bible College – I gained a husband.) We both have grown up children from our previous lives before we were saved and decided to have no more, as we want to focus on serving the Lord now. So recently when I dreamt that I was pregnant, I was horrified and even more so when I found that Gerry was not the father. I was so afraid and confused. People were telling me whom they thought the father was, but I couldn't remember doing anything with this man, or with any other man, for that matter. This was a nightmare. Was I going crazy? How could this be? In the dream, one of the pastors of our church had offered to be there when I broke the news to Gerry, and as I waited for him, I was beside myself with fear. (Even as I write about this I can feel the sheer terror that I felt in the dream, it was so real.) What would Gerry say? Would he believe me? Would he divorce me in disgust? It would hurt him so much … I didn't want to hurt him, I loved him! And what would other people say? I wasn't a bad person; I hadn't done anything wrong. What was my future going to be like now? Was this the end of everything? At this point in the dream, I woke up, with real tears streaming down my face and a question on my heart, "Lord , what was all that about?" When the Lord speaks to you in a dream, somehow you *know*. You may not understand it, but you do *know* it's from Him, so the best thing to do is ask Him. "What does it mean? What are You saying to me?"Then I remembered Mary and related her story to my dream. I suddenly realised how she must have felt. She could have been stoned to death for this. The *only* way that she could possibly have trusted God in this was if she really *knew* Him. The *only* way she could believe what the angel had said and that she was chosen for this awesome destiny was by *knowing* her God. And even then, she could only fulfil the word when the Holy Spirit came upon her and overshadowed her. This was a life-long commitment that Mary was making and there was no backing out once the decision was made. She didn't know what the future was going to be like, or if she could cope with it. This was a breathtaking responsibility, to give birth to the Son of God, to bring Him into the world, to teach Him and watch Him grow to maturity. But Mary did know her God, and she knew that He was a faithful God. If He said it, then He would watch over His word to perform it. She was humble enough to know that she couldn't do it on her own, but wise enough to believe that with God nothing is impossible. The Word of God says,

'Trust in the LORD with all your heart and lean not on your own understanding; in all your ways acknowledge (know) him, and he will make your paths straight.' Proverbs 3:5. *'If you do not stand firm in your faith, you will not stand at all.'* Isaiah 7:9.

Mary knew that it was not by her own might or power but by His Spirit alone. When God speaks a word, He always confirms and encourages, and for Mary it was no different. She immediately acted on His word, got ready and went to see her relative Elizabeth, and there God's word was confirmed.

> *'At that time Mary got ready and hurried to a town in the hill country of Judea, where she entered Zechariah's home and greeted Elizabeth. When Elizabeth heard Mary's greeting, the baby leapt in her womb, and Elizabeth was filled with the Holy Spirit. In a loud voice she exclaimed: "Blessed are you among women, and blessed is the child you will bear! But why am I so favoured, that the mother of my Lord should come to me? As soon as the sound of your greeting reached my ears, the baby in my womb leaped for joy. Blessed is she who has believed that what the Lord has said to her will be accomplished!"*
> Luke 1:39–45.

"The mother of my Lord ... Blessed is she who has believed that what the Lord has said to her will be accomplished ..." So Elizabeth knew too. It wasn't all in Mary's imagination. It was really true. Greatly encouraged, she burst into a song of praise and thanks, further confirming that she believed and accepted God's will for her life.

> Luke 1:46–55. *"My soul glorifies the Lord*
> *and my spirit rejoices in God my Saviour,*
> *for he has been mindful of the humble state*
> *   of his servant.*
> *From now on all generations will call me blessed,*

for the Mighty One has done great things for
me – holy is his name.
His mercy extends to those who fear him,
from generation to generation.
He has performed mighty deeds with his arm;
he has scattered those who are proud in their
inmost thoughts.
He has brought down rulers from their thrones
but has lifted up the humble.
He has filled the hungry with good things
but has sent the rich away empty.
He has helped His servant Israel,
remembering to be merciful
to Abraham and his descendants for ever,
even as he said to our fathers."

You can almost feel the sense of excitement and wonder in Mary as she sings. She hasn't yet seen the fulfilment of the word physically, but because she sees it all in her spirit, she can thank God in advance because she *knows*. Knows that He is God, He is her Saviour. Knows that He's not chosen her because of any great thing she has done, but simply through His grace. She has surrendered to Him. His arm is not too short and nothing is impossible for Him. She knew the history of her nation, of what God had done before and the promises that He had made. He is a faithful God. He *does* watch over His word to perform it. His mercy *does* extend to those who fear Him ... and Mary feared God. Many years ago, 16th December 1951 to be precise, in a city called Leicester in England, another baby girl was born. No-one knew the destiny that was in store for this little girl either, but God had a plan for her life also. On Sunday 27th September 1987, at the age of 35, she too was confronted with the truth of God's word: 'Jesus is the Son of God and He died for *me.*' Was she willing to accept this or refuse? She was a single mother with a broken marriage and a string of broken relationships, and she'd messed up her life in so many ways. Was it really possible that there was a God up there who really cared about *her*, who wanted *her?* Something stirred in her ... she *wanted* to believe. She *had* to believe and so was born again into a new life with Jesus. That little girl, that woman, was me and on that day I stepped right into the loving arms of Jesus and into God's plan for me. I dared to say yes, and now all I have to do is walk in it. The Bible says, *"For I know the plans I have for you," declares the Lord, "plans to prosper you and not to harm you, plans to give you hope and a future."* Jer.29:11.

God has a plan for your life, a plan that is as awesome as the plan He had for Mary. Mary dared to say yes to God's plan, and she showed by being willing to give her whole self that she loved the Lord with all her heart, soul, mind and strength, fulfilling the first and greatest commandment. She chose to move into the fullness of what God had for her, leaving her own plans behind, to go higher and deeper in total surrender, intimacy ... she conceived Jesus by the Holy Spirit and carried Him in her being as He grew in her, until she gave birth to Him into the world. *'The Word became flesh'.* God took what she willingly gave – probably the only thing that she owned – her virginity, and made it into the greatest weapon against Satan that the world will ever know. God's plan for you is the same: to go higher and deeper into a more intimate relationship with Him, surrendering your plans to receive the fullness of His plans, knowing that He knows best. Is He truly the *Lord* of your life? Jesus said, " *... no-one can see the kingdom of God unless he is born* *again,"* John 3:3, and *" ... no-one can enter the kingdom of God unless he is born of water and the Spirit. Flesh gives birth to flesh, but the Spirit gives birth to spirit."* John 3:5–6. This refers to God's Holy Spirit. *'For God so loved the world that he gave his one and only Son, that whoever believes in him shall not perish but have eternal life.'* John 3:16. Jesus is the Way to God, the Truth of God and the Life of God. If you have accepted the truth of Jesus and invited Him into your heart, then you are born again into a new life with Him. His life is *in* you by His Spirit. Jesus lives *in* you and *you* also, like Mary, need to give birth to Him into the world. He was born of Mary, to seek and save the lost, and has not changed His purpose. Mary could not do this without the Holy Spirit's power and neither can we. This is the purpose for which you were chosen, but I emphasise again that you *cannot* live this life without the help of the Holy Spirit.

2

Married?

Not long after I'd had the dream about being pregnant, I had another dream. I was in Uganda at the time, and in this dream, I was going on a journey, so I went to the doctor to get some malaria tablets. He gave me the prescription and I went home. After some discussion, I realised that I didn't have enough of these tablets and I needed to go back to ask him for more. The doctor's waiting room was full when I arrived and I didn't feel I could wait, so I walked straight past everyone, knocked on his door and went in. As I spoke with the doctor, he leaned over his desk and with a concerned look on his face, he quietly asked me a very strange question. "So this is not your husband that you are going with, then?" His question surprised me. What did he mean? "Er.. well … er … he's my boyfriend," came my confused reply. "Oh, er.. no, just a minute, no, he is my husband … I married him. I remember now, I married him. Yes that's right, he's my husband." The doctor looked a bit doubtful at my reply, but gave me the prescription anyway. On leaving the surgery, I saw two people whom I'd spoken with before, a man and a woman. They wanted to come back with me to meet my husband, so we went to our pick-up trucks. The woman came with me in my vehicle and the man followed in his. That was the end of the dream and I woke up. What a strange dream! Again I asked, "Lord, what was that one all about?"

The dream was about God's heart for His people. The doctor represents God our Father. Many people are going to church and to God just to receive the tablets they need for the journey. They go because that's what they're supposed to do. We're supposed to take a course of malaria tablets when we go on a trip to Uganda. We're supposed to go to church when we are Christians … Aren't we? That's where we meet with God … isn't it? We go there to receive what we need from God, knowing, quite rightly, that He is the source. We get fed with the Word and encouraged, and we may receive prayer for healing or whatever else we need, then we go home again. Next week we return for more to keep us going, to keep us safe on the journey. In the dream, when I went back to the doctor, the waiting room was full of people waiting for something to happen, waiting for the doctor to call them and give them what they needed, not daring to go straight in, in case it was not their time, or because they didn't believe that he would want to be bothered with them as he was much too busy. Our churches are full of people who are going through the motions of being Christians. They faithfully go to church and maybe even attend a Bible study or a house group. They may be part of a very lively and charismatic church, where they love to sing and dance together and where there are possibly even very powerful moves of God, just as the people in the waiting room were having lively and interesting conversations and being given effective medicine. These Christians are saved but are not doing anything with the gift God has given them – Jesus. They are in religion, sitting in their chairs or pews and waiting for God to call them or supernaturally do something without any real effort on their part. If we really want something, we will reach out for it and use it.

'Therefore, brothers, since we have confidence (boldness) to enter the Most Holy Place by the blood of Jesus, by a new and living way opened for us through the curtain, that is, his body, and since we have a great priest over the house of God, let us draw near to God with a sincere heart in full assurance of faith, having our hearts sprinkled to cleanse us from a guilty conscience and having our bodies washed with pure water. Let us hold unswervingly to the hope we profess, for he who promised is faithful.'
Heb. 10:19–23.

When Jesus died on the cross, the curtain was torn in two and the way was opened for us to go right into the presence of God, to draw near to Him and receive all that His Word says we can have. It's ours for the taking. In the dream, I couldn't wait and made the decision to go straight in, confident that I could have what I came for. The doctor realised, as I told him what I needed, that something wasn't quite right, and I gave the impression that I was going away with a boyfriend rather than my husband. His question confused me and made me wonder what the truth was, and I realised that *'yes he was'* my husband; I *had* married him and even had it in writing. If you have accepted Jesus Christ into your life, if you are born again into a new life with Him, then you are the 'Bride' of Christ. He is your *Husband*. Many Christians are treating Jesus like a boyfriend, meeting with Him sometimes for a date when they feel like it and it's convenient. They may think they love Him, but they don't really *know* Him, they only know *about* Him. Jesus wants an intimate relationship, a oneness, with us. He wants the spiritual marriage to be consummated by the Holy Spirit. We need to realise and believe that He really is our husband and loves us passionately to the extent that He has even put it in writing.

When a couple are married, they go through a wedding ceremony and are legally man and wife, but it's not a complete marriage until it is consummated. Then the couple have to live together and the intimacy and love continue and grow. It takes time and effort to really get to know the other person. It's the same when we become Christians, but often, because of things that have happened in our lives previously, we hold back through fear. That's how it was for me. Because of things that had happened to me before I became a Christian, I was a bit afraid of what I'd let myself in for and there was no way that I could bow down and worship a 'he'. I had built a big thick wall around me that no one was going to penetrate, and I suppose you could say I was spiritually frigid. It took a while for the Lord to knock the wall down and for me to learn to trust Him. I praise God that He is so loving and patient. I had noticed that some of the other Christians whom I knew seemed to have something more than I had, a kind of fire in their relationship with God, a *life*. They seemed much closer to Him and they also spoke in tongues. I wanted to get to know God better and I realised that I couldn't do it on my own, so if what they had would help me, then I *wanted* it.

They told me that it was the baptism of the Holy Spirit, and all I had to do was ask for it. This sounded simple enough, so I asked … and I asked … others prayed with me … and I asked again, but nothing seemed to happen. Each time I asked, I became more and more disappointed, feeling totally rejected. What was wrong with me? Was I not good enough? How come others could receive this gift and not me? … Then one day I read these words in a little booklet: 'Have you accepted Jesus as Lord of your life?' The words seemed to jump from the page and I couldn't get past them. 'Have you accepted Jesus as Lord of your life?' "What a stupid thing to ask," I thought. "I'm a Christian, aren't I?" As I read the words over and over again, they seemed to change into 'Have you accepted Jesus as *Lord* of your life?' The emphasis was on *Lord* and I suddenly realised that I had accepted Jesus *into* my life but I hadn't allowed Him to be *Lord.* He gave His whole self for me, but I had not given *myself* to *Him.* I wanted to stay in control. A good marriage is *always* a two-way thing. I promptly gave myself to God in prayer, and shortly after this attended a Christian conference in Dundee, Scotland, where I really believed something special was going to happen. It did – *after* the *last* meeting, on the *last* day when it seemed as if everything had finished, when I thought that it was too late. God's timing is always right. He's never late, and He's always prompt. An American lady by the name of Shari Moon, the wife of one of the speakers, came over and introduced herself. She prayed for me and finally after almost three years as a Christian, I received the baptism of the Holy Spirit and the gift of tongues. I'll never forget the little skip that Shari had in her step when I received this gift. Suddenly the flowers seemed brighter, I went into raptures over the sky and the Scriptures came alive. I felt accepted and far more 'at one' with my Jesus. The marriage was consummated and now I could really get to know Him.

So, coming back to the doctor's surgery, I had boldly entered right into his presence, regardless of what anyone else thought. From that place I received not only what I went for but also the revelation that I had a husband and not just a boyfriend, which meant that I could now live in that revelation. Everything, absolutely everything, everything, everything we need comes from God's presence and our relationship with Him through Jesus. God is preparing His bride. We are being equipped and matured to be co-heirs with Christ and to share His heart, His home and His throne forever. We are His inheritance. Isn't that an amazing thought? We have an inheritance in Him, but He also has an inheritance in us (see Eph.1:14 and 18).As the bride of Christ, we are drawn into a deeper and more intimately passionate relationship with Jesus, which cannot be hidden. When you're in love, you glow and it shows. In the dream, after I had received the revelation that it was my husband with whom I was going on the journey, other people wanted to come with me to meet him, and the pick-up trucks speak for themselves. This is *revival,* and without doubt, by the grace of God, revival is coming, and that revival begins with … YOU.

As I quoted earlier, the Bible says, *"For I know the plans I have for you," declares the Lord, "plans to prosper you and not to harm you, plans to give you hope and a future."* Jer.29:11.

But the Bible also says that we have all sinned and fallen short of the glory of God (see Rom.3:23). In other words, we have turned away from God's best for us, *His plan.* When we were born again, we received the fullness of God's plan for our lives and entered into the marriage, but because we don't really know Jesus very well yet, we're not really living in the reality of His love or in the fullness of what He's given us. Imagine being given a gift. A large box, beautifully wrapped with a ribbon and a big bow on the top. It looks good and it's been offered to *you* … but *you* have to take it. It's not really yours until you receive it. *Then* you still don't know what you've been given until you take off

14

the wrapping and look inside. You have been given the gift of Jesus, all of Him, a loving Husband, and an inheritance through Him, but as with every marriage, you then have to get to know what and whom you have been given. My heart as you continue to read this book is that your heart will be stirred with a desire to know the Lord in a more intimate way, that you will be drawn deeper into His loving arms and into His presence, in total surrender to *His* plan for your life and for the whole of mankind.

> God is preparing His bride. *'I saw the Holy City, the new Jerusalem, coming down out of heaven from God, prepared as a bride beautifully dressed for her husband.'* Rev.21:2.

God is building His church, His temple where His glory will be contained and revealed.

Do you want to contain and reveal the glory of God? To be His temple?

Are you willing to allow God to work it in you and to build?

Do you really want revival? … Even with all it will cost you? God is willing if you are, and He is able to do immeasurably more than all you can ask or imagine, but it's according to *His* power working in you (see Eph.3:20). And the cost of this? … your life.

3

Oh, My Goodness!

So what about this glory, what actually is it that we fell short of and turned our backs on? If we are God's temple, as the Bible says we are, and the temple is to contain and reveal His glory, then we need to know what it is, where to find it and how to reveal it. Is it *really* there inside *me*?

> *'When Moses went up on the mountain, the cloud covered it, and the glory of the LORD settled on Mount Sinai. For six days the cloud covered the mountain, and on the seventh day the LORD called to Moses from within the cloud. To the Israelites the glory of the LORD looked like a consuming fire on top of the mountain.'* Exodus 24:15–17.

Mount Sinai is often called the mountain of God because it was the place where Moses met with God, where God spoke with him face to face and where He gave him the Ten Commandments and instructions for building the Tabernacle. We see in these verses that the 'glory' was in a cloud at the top of the mountain. God Himself was within the cloud, and so I believe that we can safely say that the 'glory' is, in fact, the presence of God. To the Israelites, the glory looked like a consuming fire. According to the dictionary, to 'consume' means to 'reduce to nothing or burn up'. When we enter into the presence of God, all that is not pure is burned up. God is a Holy God and *cannot* look upon sin and in His presence we become as nothing. The focus is all on Him. In 1Tim.6:16, Paul speaks of God ' ... *who lives in unapproachable light, whom no-one has seen or can see.'* The cloud is not the glory, but the cloud covers it for our protection.

Moving on to Exodus chapter 33, God had instructed Moses to take the children of Israel into the land that He had promised them on oath through Abraham, Isaac and Jacob. For their own sakes, however, He would not go with them because they were a stiff-necked people, that is, they were unresponsive and sinful, and He might destroy them. Instead, He would send an angel before them to drive out their enemies. As we read on, there are a number of verses which are relevant to our theme. *'Now Moses used to take a tent and pitch it outside the camp some distance away, calling it the "tent of meeting".'* (Verse 7). *'As Moses went into the tent, the pillar of cloud would come down and stay at the entrance, while the LORD spoke with Moses.'* (Verse 9). *'The LORD would speak to Moses face to face, as a man speaks with his friend.'* (Verse 11). In the glory of God, we can speak with Him "face to face" and intercede for others as Moses did.

'Moses said to the Lord, "You have been telling me, 'Lead these people,' but you have not let me know whom you will send with me. You have said, 'I know you by name and you have found favour with me.' ... ... If you are pleased with me, teach me your ways so I may know you and continue to find favour with you. Remember that this nation is your people." The LORD replied, "My Presence will go with you, and I will give you rest."' (Verses 12 – 14). Again here we see that the 'glory' is the presence of God and in this presence we can boldly come before Him, be totally open about how we

feel, remind Him of the things that He has said before – not that He's forgotten – and ask for what we want and need. This is also the place where we learn and find out what God's will is. You cannot have your own agenda in the presence of God because that is rebellion, and rebellion is sin. Total submission to God's will is necessary. "May it be to me as you have said," were Mary's words. We also see here that in God's presence He gives us rest and peace.

'Then Moses said to him, "If your Presence does not go with us, do not send us up from here. How will anyone know that you are pleased with me and with your people unless you go with us? What else will distinguish me and your people from all the other people on the face of the earth?"' (Verse 15). There was no way that Moses wanted to go anywhere without God. Many years previously he had tried to work out God's plan for him in his own strength, but had painfully learned that it didn't work, so now he *knew* that without God, he could do nothing. He was totally reliant on the Lord. If we are walking in the presence of God, in His will, then we will be seen to be different. People need to see that you have something that they don't have, something that's worth having. We are called to be set apart for God, a holy people, belonging to God, loved by Him and blessed.

Some time ago, while I was working in a shopping centre promoting kitchens, my new supervisor came to visit me. After a while she said, "You seem to keep yourself quite well motivated and cheerful while you're on the stand." "I suppose I do, I hadn't really thought about it much," was my reply. There was a pause, and then she said, "You seem to have a sort of glow about you," to which my immediate response was, "Oh, that's Jesus." Another pause, then somewhat nervously she asked, "Will you pray for me?" What a question! "Of course I will, what would you like me to pray

19

for you?" I asked. Then she said the most amazing thing, "I want what you've got." Praise the Lord! That's the sort of evangelism I like. I have noticed that whenever I've spent time in the presence of the Lord and studying His Word, things like this seem to happen and people are attracted. It's not me, it's Jesus shining through me. You see, when we have been with the Lord it *will* show, just as it did with Moses. *'When Moses came down from Mount Sinai with the two tablets of the Testimony in his hands, he was not aware that his face was radiant because he had spoken with the LORD.'* Exodus 34:29. In Exodus 33:17, we read, *'And the Lord said to Moses, "I will do the very thing you have asked, because I am pleased with you and I know you by name."'* God saw Moses' heart. Hebrews 11:6 says, *'Without faith it is impossible to please God, because anyone who comes to him must believe that he exists and that he rewards those who earnestly seek him.'* In the presence of God, as you begin to know Him, your prayers *are* answered. *'Then Moses said, "Now show me your glory." And the LORD said, "I will cause all my goodness to pass in front of you, and I will proclaim my name, the LORD, in your presence. I will have mercy on whom I will have mercy, and I will have compassion on whom I will have compassion. But," he said, "you cannot see my face, for no-one may see me and live."'* (Verses 18–20).

"I will cause all my goodness to pass in front of you." The glory of God is His *goodness,* and when you see His *goodness*, really see it, even if only in part, *then* He truly can become the Lord of your life. *"I will proclaim my name, the LORD, in your presence."* The 'name' represents the very nature, character and person of God, and here implies His mercy and His compassion. God said, "*I will cause ... I will proclaim ... I will ... "* *He* will do it, a divine work of God

– if we are surrendered to His will. God created human beings, not puppets. We do have freedom of choice, His will or ours. *"You cannot see my face, for no-one may see me and live."* Our God is an awesome God. If He were to reveal the fullness of His glory, we would die on the spot. The glory is when He unveils everything that makes Him God, and the light of that would be too great for us. In Acts, chapter nine, when Paul (or Saul as he was then) had his Damascus Road experience, he was confronted with a bright light which caused him to fall to the ground and blinded him. He describes it in Acts 26 as brighter than the noonday sun. In a hot dry climate, the noonday sun is extremely bright, more than we can bear to look at. In the days of His humanity, Jesus was not seen in His glory. John had lived with Jesus for three years, and yet in his Book of Revelation he said of the risen and ascended Jesus, *"His face was like the sun shining in all its brilliance. When I saw him, I fell at his feet as though dead."* (Rev 1:16 and 17). He *is* a consuming fire.

So in answer to Moses' request to see His glory, God replied that He would cause His *goodness* to pass by, but do we actually know what His *goodness* is? The answer follows in verses 21 onwards: *'Then the LORD said, "There is a place near me where you may stand on a rock."'*

Who is the rock on which we stand? In Matthew 16, after Simon Peter spoke out his revelation that Jesus was the Christ, the Son of the living God, Jesus said that on that rock, the revelation of truth, He would build His church. We need revelation of who Jesus is to enable us to stand on the rock. He is our firm foundation and only through Jesus can the church, the people of God, be built to contain and reveal God.

In the first chapter of the gospel of John, we read, *'In the beginning was the Word, and the Word was with God and the Word was God. He was with God in the beginning,'* and then in verse 14, *'The Word became flesh and made his dwelling among us.'* John was writing about Jesus, who was with God from the beginning, and after His resurrection from the dead He returned to be seated at God's right hand where He is *near* to God.

> *"There is a place near me where you may stand on a rock."* Returning to Exodus 33, verses 22 – 23, *"When my glory passes by, I will put you in a cleft in the rock and cover you with my hand until I have passed by. Then I will remove my hand and you will see my back; but my face must not be seen."*

"When my glory passes by … " Out of the goodness of God's heart, He sent His one and only Son to die for us on the cross, to make the way for us to know Him. At the time of this conversation between God and Moses, although the Saviour was both planned and promised, He had not yet come. Jesus *is* the very *goodness* of God, the nature and character of God. So if Jesus is the *goodness* of God and the goodness is the *glory,* then, *"When my glory passes by … "* – when Jesus passed by on this earth – *"I will put you in the cleft of the rock … ".* 'Therefore, if anyone is in Christ, he is a new creation: the old has gone, the new has come! All this is from God, who reconciled us to himself through Christ …' 2 Corinthians 5:17–18.

If we have accepted Jesus as our Saviour, then we are 'in' Him (the Rock) by the grace of God. *" … and cover you with my hand … "* The blood of Jesus covers you and He is the right hand of God that reaches down into a hurting world and saves us. He cleansed me from my sins by His blood and made me totally acceptable in God's sight.

'Blessed are they whose transgressions are forgiven, whose sins are covered.' Rom. 4:7.

'Sing to the LORD a new song, for he has done marvellous things; his right hand and his holy arm have worked salvation for him.' Psalm 98:1. *"Then I will remove my hand and you will see my back."*

After Jesus had risen from the dead and returned to the Father, the Holy Spirit came and we were able to see what God had done, as when He passed by Moses. Only by the power of the Holy Spirit are we able to see the goodness of God, His 'glory'.

And only through Jesus can we see God. *'No-one has ever seen God, but God the One and Only, who is at the Father's side, has made him known.'* John 1:18. *'Anyone who has seen me has seen the Father.'* John 14:9. *" ... but my face must not be seen."* No-one on this earth can see the face of God and live. Only in the Holy City shall we see Him face to face. *'No longer will there be any curse. The throne of God and of the Lamb will be in the city, and his servants will serve him. They will see his face, and his name will be on their foreheads.'* Revelation 22:3–4.

It is only through Christ that we can have the knowledge of the glory of God and we can only *see* His glory if we stand on this rock and take shelter in Him. *'This is love: not that we loved God, but that he loved us and sent his Son as an atoning sacrifice for our sins.. ... . No-one has ever seen God; but if we love one another, God lives in us and his love is made complete in us. We know that we live in him and he in us, because he has given us his Spirit.'* 1 John 4:10–13.

The questions that we asked were: What is this glory that we fell short of, or turned away from? Where can I find it? Is it really there inside me? And if it is, how do I contain and reveal it?In a nutshell, the glory is the presence of God and the goodness of God, in the form of Jesus Christ. Jesus is God, so when human beings turn away from God and go their own way instead of His, they turn away from His best for them, His goodness. You only have to look around you at the world today to see the effects of man going his way instead of God's way. Jesus came that we may have life, life in all its abundance. When we receive Jesus as our Saviour, He comes to live in our hearts by His Holy Spirit. He *is* the glory, so that means that the glory *must* be in us. The goodness of God and the presence of God are there in us; everything we need is there. To reveal the glory, you need God's revelation to you of Jesus, who He is and what it is that you have inherited through Him. You can only live in His goodness when you realise that you have it. The only way for this to happen is to choose to believe and then get to know Him. He *is* the Way, the Truth and the Life.

'[For I always pray to] the God of our Lord Jesus Christ, the Father of glory, that He may grant you a spirit of wisdom and revelation [of insight into mysteries and secrets] in the [deep and intimate] knowledge of Him,

By having the eyes of your heart flooded with light, so that you can know and understand the hope to which He has called you, and how rich is His glorious inheritance in the saints (His set apart ones).

And [so that you can know and understand] what is the immeasurable and unlimited and surpassing greatness of His power in and for us who believe, as demonstrated in the working of His mighty strength,

Which He exerted in Christ when He raised Him from the dead and seated Him at His [own] right hand in the heavenly [places].' Ephesians 1:17–20 Amplified Bible. *'When they saw the courage of Peter and John and realised that they were unschooled, ordinary men, they were astonished and they took note that these men had been with Jesus.'* Acts 4:13.

4

A Place to Meet with God

The Way

Over a period of a few months, the Lord gave me a series of four visions which I will describe later, but first I want to tell you of the things that God revealed to me about the Tabernacle, so that you will see more clearly what He was showing me. God's heart has always been, and still is, to live and dwell in the midst of His people, and so during forty days and forty nights in the presence of the Lord on Mount Sinai in the cloud of God's glory (see Ex. 24:18), Moses was given instructions of how this would be possible.

> *"Then have them make a sanctuary for me, and I will dwell among them. Make the tabernacle and all its furnishings exactly like the pattern I will show you."* Ex. 25:8–9.

The term 'sanctuary' denotes 'holy place', a place set apart for God. In the Tabernacle, or tent of meeting, we have a foreshadowing of what was to come, a picture of all that would be fulfilled in Jesus. It was vital that the tabernacle and all its furnishings be made *exactly* to the instructions given by God. Every detail was to symbolise the majesty and holiness of Jesus and to show the way for man to safely enter into the presence of a perfectly holy and awesome

God. So let me take you now on a journey into the 'Holy of Holies', into the presence of our Lord where the 'glory' is. There really is *no* other way, only His way, with no short-cuts.

> *'The LORD said to Moses, "Tell the Israelites to bring me an offering. You are to receive the offering for me from each man whose heart prompts him to give. These are the offerings you are to receive from them: gold, silver and bronze; blue, purple and scarlet yarn and fine linen; goat hair; ram skins dyed red and hides of sea cows; acacia wood; olive oil for the light; spices for the anointing oil and for the fragrant incense; and onyx stones and other gems to be mounted on the ephod and breastpiece"'*
> Exodus 25:1–7.

This first temple, known as the Tabernacle, was built using materials given by the people willingly and from their hearts. This demonstrates to us that to enter into the presence of God, there must be a desire not only for what we can *receive from* God, but also a desire to *give to* Him, not because we *have* to give but because we *want* to give. These were specific items that would be needed for the building of the tabernacle, things which God requested and not simply items that people wanted to get rid of. How often we give to God things for which we have no more use, the time we have left over or simply what *we* want to give or what *we think* He wants, instead of listening and learning what it is He really desires. Many people do wonderful charitable and loving works and think that because they are 'good' people, this will get them to heaven, but of course this is not the case. If it is not what God is asking, then we are acting in independence and rebellion, and rebellion is sin. The Bible tells us that the *only* way to the Father is through the Son (see John 14:6). We are not God, *He* is, and it has to be *His* way, not ours. We cannot manipulate God or find our own way to Him. It is presumptuous of us to think we know best. We must follow the *exact* plan that He gives us. The tabernacle is constructed of three parts, just as we are made up of three parts. The 'Outer Court' relates to our body, which is exposed to the elements and where there is less protection from worldly influences. The 'Holy Place' represents our soul, which is in turn made up of three things: mind, will and emotions. The 'Holy of Holies' represents our spirit, the place where we meet with God, His Spirit and our spirit. It is the whole person that our Father wants not just one or two sections. We enter into the Outer Court on the east side (see diagram on page 192), and first we come to is the altar of sacrifice, where the animal sacrifices were carried out to make atonement (at-one-ment) with God. This represents the cross of Jesus, where the ultimate sacrifice was made. In our journey to the presence of God, this is the first thing with which we are confronted: the blood of Jesus Christ that was shed for us. He gave His life to make the way for us to come into the presence of God, so when we come to the altar of sacrifice, we need to lay down our own lives. In other words, we decide to go God's way instead of ours. This is where we are born again into a new life and our old life is crucified with Jesus, burnt up on the altar.

'I have been crucified with Christ and I no longer live, but Christ lives in me. The life I live in the body, I live by faith in the Son of God, who loved me and gave himself for me.' Gal. 2:20.

This is also a daily event. *"If anyone would come after me, he must deny himself and take up his cross daily and follow me. For whoever wants to save his life will lose it, but whoever loses his life for me will save it." Luke 9:23–24.* If we hold on to 'self', we will miss out on living in the fullness of the life that Jesus has for us.

Before I became a Christian, after my divorce, I drifted into one relationship after another, searching for love. I wanted to believe that there was someone who could love me. The trouble was that, like many people in the world, I was looking for the wrong kind of love. I was looking for what the world sees as love, but which I realise now was not real love at all. As each of these relationships went wrong, I became more and more hurt and rejected until I reached a point where I just couldn't take any more and decided I was better off on my own. I had my daughter Keeli, a successful business and a nice house. I could take care of myself … Who was I kidding? … It wasn't until I met Jesus that I discovered what real love is, and on that day I wept, because suddenly He was there with me. It was as though He had wrapped His arms around me and was holding me close saying, "It's alright, I'm here, and you can give me all the past, give me all the pain and rejection and the loneliness. Let go of it, I'm here. I love you." Some years later, during my days at YWAM (Youth With A Mission), we'd had a whole week of meetings where people were laughing for joy, and they really *seemed* to be meeting with God. I longed to join in and be a part of what was happening, but all I ever seemed to do was cry. I felt rejected again and shied away even from being prayed for. Early on the Friday morning of that week, during my quiet time with the Lord, I felt prompted to forgive all the people who had hurt me in the past for whatever reason. Then later that day, during the meeting, I found myself in the midst of a group of people receiving prayer. After a while, a man named Bill said, "Rose, I know your name is *Rose* White (before I married Gerry, my surname was White), but I believe the Lord is saying that you are *Snow* White." At this I burst into tears, as I realised that the Lord had forgiven me for my past. I had been washed as white as snow.

The Bible says, *"And when you stand praying, if you hold anything against anyone, forgive him, so that your Father in heaven may forgive you your sins."* Mark 11:25.

As I had forgiven those who had hurt me, I was able to *receive* His forgiveness and healing for myself, and also to forgive myself.

"Come now, let us reason together," says the LORD. "Though your sins are like scarlet, they shall be as white as snow." Isaiah 1:18.

As my friends continued to pray for me, I wept, and then I noticed that there was a smell in the room, a revolting smell, like a sewer or something. The smell grew stronger and stronger as the minutes passed, until it was so strong that it was almost knocking me out, and yet strangely no-one else seemed to even notice it. How on earth could they miss it, it was *so* strong? Eventually, I found the situation so funny, that everyone was being so super polite and pretending they hadn't noticed, that I burst out laughing and asked, "What is that awful smell?" They all looked at me in amazement, because no-one else could smell anything … The Lord was allowing me to smell the corpse that I had been dragging

31

around. I was a new creation, the old person had gone, but I hadn't let go. I was holding onto the old life with all its hurts and dragging it around with me. The Lord was saying, "Let go, it stinks and it's weighing you down so that you are not free to receive what I have for you." On the day I was born again, I was totally forgiven and accepted, but I hadn't received the revelation of God's forgiveness, and so this was restricting me from receiving. I cried when He called me 'Snow White', because at that moment, I was confronted with what Jesus had done for me on the cross. Jesus didn't die for us to stay at the moment of our conversion. He wants us to go further, beyond the cross, to unwrap the gift that He has given us.

Returning to the Tabernacle and moving on from the altar of sacrifice, which represents the cross, as we draw nearer to the presence of God, we come to the 'Bronze Laver' or basin.

> *'Then the LORD said to Moses, "Make a bronze basin, with its bronze stand, for washing. Place it between the Tent of Meeting and the altar, and put water in it … Aaron and his sons are to wash their hands and feet with water from it. Whenever they enter the Tent of Meeting, they shall wash with water so that they will not die. Also, when they approach the altar to minister by presenting an offering made to the LORD by fire, they shall wash their hands and feet so that they will not die."'* Exodus 30:17–21.

Aaron and his sons were instructed to wash their hands and feet at this laver *every* time they went into the Tabernacle, as part of the ceremonial cleansing of the priests. They had to be pure to enter the presence of God. '*Who may ascend the*

hill of the LORD?
Who may stand in his holy place? He who has clean
hands and a pure heart.' Psalm 24:3–4.

The laver represents our baptism, as an outward sign and pledge, or promise, of an inward repentance, a turning back to God. Baptism in the Name of Jesus is like a seal of the new relationship of belonging to Him and being committed to Him. '... *for all of you who were baptised into Christ have clothed yourselves with Christ.* Galatians 3:27. It is a pictorial representation showing that we have died to our old life and have risen again to a new one. Baptism demonstrates that we are washed clean and can enter into the Holy Place, and something we need to remind ourselves of regularly. When we are born again, we are washed completely clean but it is also necessary, figuratively speaking, that *whenever* we approach the altar to minister to the Lord, we wash our hands and feet by keeping a short account with Him of our sins so as not to be tainted spiritually. We sin when we do what we want instead of what God wants.The laver was made up using the mirrors of the women who served at the entrance to the Tent of Meeting. Mirrored glass was unknown in those times, so highly polished bronze was used. Mirrors are used to focus on self and so the laver also represents that you willingly renounce glorifying yourself in exchange for service to God.

5

A Place to Meet with God

It's the Truth

The next stage of our journey into the presence of God is through the Holy Place, where there were three items of furniture. The Lampstand stood on one side, the Table for the Bread of the Presence on the opposite side, and the Altar of Incense was situated in front of the curtain leading into the Holy of Holies. All three are of equal importance if we are to enter into God's glorious presence, and you cannot have one without the others. The Table for the 'Bread of the Presence' or 'Showbread' was made from acacia wood and covered with pure gold and upon it were placed twelve loaves of bread, in two rows of six, one for each tribe of Israel, – God's people.

'This bread is to be set out before the LORD regularly, Sabbath after Sabbath, on behalf of the Israelites, as a lasting covenant. It belongs to Aaron and his sons, who are to eat it in a holy place, because it is a most holy part of their regular share of the offerings made to the LORD by fire'. Leviticus 24;8–9 Jesus said, *"I am the bread of life. Your forefathers ate the manna in the desert, yet they died. But here is the bread that comes down from heaven, which a man may eat and not die. I am the living bread that came down from*

*heaven. If anyone eats of this bread, he will live for
ever. This bread is my flesh, which I will give for the
life of the world."* John 6: 48–51.

Jesus is the Word that became flesh and God has given us
His Word, so we need to 'eat' it. How do we do this? ... By
reading about Him in His written word and getting to know
Him *in a holy place*, that is, during time set apart for Him.
This is *a most holy part* of our *regular share of the offerings
to the Lord*. Regular times with the Lord, reading and
studying His Word, are so important. In the old covenant,
only the priests ate the bread, now as born again Christians,
we are all chosen as priests to come before the Lord and eat.
Psalm 23 tells us that the Lord has prepared a table before
us. He has prepared a feast, a feast of His Word. If our desire
is to *know* the Lord, one of the things that we *must* do is to
come to the table and eat. As the body of Jesus was broken
for us on the cross, and the bread is broken, so also our will
has to be broken before we can enter into God's presence.
We have to say, "Not my way, but Yours Lord."

Reading the Word of God and getting to know about Him
is in itself, not enough. Bread can be dry. We need help and
revelation, given in the light of the Holy Spirit, to bring life
to the written word. The Lampstand, with its pure oil to keep
it burning, represents the baptism of the Holy Spirit, which
gives spiritual understanding of what God's Word says and
power to live it. The Word and the Holy Spirit work together.
It can be no other way. There were no windows in the
Tabernacle, so the Golden Lampstand lit the way. It was
positioned facing the Table and they were both set at an
equal distance from the Holy of Holies, showing that they
were of equal importance into the presence of God. Bearing
in mind that things in the Old Testament are revealed in the

New and are often prophetic of things to come, either now or in the future, I am reminded of John's vision of the new heaven and earth.

'There will be no more night. They will not need the light of a lamp or the light of the sun, for the Lord God will give them light.' Revelation 22:5.

Jesus said, *"I am the light of the world. Whoever follows me will never walk in darkness, but will have the light of life."* John 8:12. What is the 'light of life'? *'In the last days, God says, I will pour out my Spirit on all people. Your sons and daughters will prophesy, your young men will see visions, your old men will dream dreams. Even my servants, both men and women, I will pour out my Spirit in those days, and they will prophesy.'* Acts 2:17–18.

In the first chapter of Acts, after He had risen from the dead, Jesus showed Himself to His disciples and gave them this command: *"Do not leave Jerusalem, but wait for the gift my Father promised, which you heard me speak about. For John baptised with water, but in a few days you will be baptised with the Holy Spirit,"* and *" ... you will receive power when the Holy Spirit comes on you."*

When Jesus was baptised by John in the River Jordan, *' ... as he was praying, heaven was opened and the Holy Spirit descended on him in bodily form like a dove.'* Luke 3:21–22. *'Jesus (was) full of the Holy Spirit ... and was led by the Spirit ... '* Luke 4:1.

Only after Jesus was filled with the Holy Spirit was He able to perform miracles. This same Holy Spirit who lived in Jesus will return to live in *all* who open their lives to His power. If *Jesus* needed this empowering, how can we dare say that we do not need it?

> *'Do not conform any longer to the pattern of this world, but be transformed by the renewing of your mind.'* Romans 12:2.

Our minds are to be as the mind of Christ and this only comes through the light of the Holy Spirit.

> *'For with you is the fountain of life; in your light we see light.'* Psalm 36:9.

The design of the Lampstand was based on that of an almond tree *with flowerlike cups, buds and blossoms* (see Exodus 25:31ff). In that part of the world, the almond tree was the first to blossom in spring, showing us that this lamp not only lights the way but also helps us to blossom and produce fruit when combined with God's Word. It was made of a single piece of pure gold consisting of six branches, three on each side, from a single stem, each holding a bowl containing oil and a wick.

> In John 15:5 we read, *" I (Jesus) am the vine; you are the branches. If a man remains in me and I in him, he will bear much fruit." 'In Christ we who are many form one body, and each member belongs to all the others.'* Romans 12:5. *'He is before all things, and in him all things hold together. And he is the head of the body, the church.'* Colossians 1:17–18

We are all joined together with Christ at the centre, and so the Lampstand's design represents unity in the body of Christ through the Holy Spirit. There were seven lamps in all, and in Jewish thought seven was the number of completion. The truth of God's Word says that we are complete in Him, but we will only know this as we allow the Holy Spirit to enlighten us. *Choose* to believe and act upon what God's Word says, and in time, you will surely *see* the truth of it. Human nature says, "You show me and then I'll believe," but God says, "No, you believe and then I'll show you."

I imagine many of you saying in frustration at this point, " I *am trying* to read the Bible, and I *have been* baptised in the Holy Spirit but I *still* find it difficult to understand what I'm reading and also I don't have much time." That is just how I felt; even though initially after I was baptised in the Holy Spirit, the Bible did seem to come alive to a certain degree, I still found it very difficult. I was a slow reader and didn't understand what I was reading, and so I found the Bible boring. I couldn't admit this to anyone, of course, because I was too embarrassed. They might think me thick, or stupid, or just lazy – which were all things that I was thinking about myself anyway, so I didn't want reminding. It was much easier to listen to the preacher on Sundays, busy myself with other things and *look* the part. I did find myself a nice easy 'Daily Reading' book with an encouraging little word for each day, so that I could at least say I was reading some of the Word. These little books are excellent and the Lord very often speaks through them, but they are not enough on their own and should never be used like a daily horoscope. Obviously, as time went on, I did learn some, but deep down I *knew* that I had to get to know God's Word better and I did honestly *want* to. In the end, prompted by the Holy Spirit, I decided, "Well if I can't do it by myself,

I will put myself in a position where I *have* to learn." – Firstly God took me to YWAM and then to Kingdom Faith Bible College. I am not saying here that everyone should go to Bible College, as that would be impossible for many, but it was there that I discovered 'The Way Of The Spirit' Bible reading course, by the late Dr. John McKay, previously Director of Studies at Kingdom Faith College. Suddenly, as I was directed through the Scriptures, they were beginning to make sense, and I was also learning to hear what the Holy Spirit was saying to *me* through them. The Bible was becoming *exciting* ... *I* was becoming excited. What I'm saying here is: "Get yourself a good Bible reading course, because as the Scriptures start to make sense to you and become more exciting, you will *want* to read them and so will find the time." When you really *want* to do something, you make time for it.

It was the duty of the priests to tend the lamp both morning and evening to keep the light burning in order that they could see where they were going, using a constant supply of clear oil of pressed olives. We also, as priests, need to tend the light every day by giving our time and attention to Jesus through the Word and prayer, including Him in everything we do, so that we can stay 'on fire' and constantly be walking in His light and His ways. Don't be like the foolish virgins who ran out of oil before the bridegroom arrived. (see Matthew 25). *'Fan into flame the gift of God, which is in you ...'* 2 Timothy 1:6. Stay focused and *'press on towards the goal to win the prize for which God has called me heavenwards in Christ Jesus.'* Philippians 3:14. As I said earlier, there is no easy way or shortcut to God's presence.

As we continue our journey through the Tabernacle with Jesus, His Word and His Spirit working together, we come to the Altar of Incense, a place of prayer and worship. *'Each one had a harp and they were holding golden bowls full of incense, which are the prayers of the saints. And they sang a new song.'* Revelation 5:8–9. This altar was positioned in front of the curtain, leading to the Holy of Holies, although in Hebrews chapter 9, the author describes it as being actually through the curtain, which shows us how important the incense is in relation to coming into the presence of God.

Prayer, praise and worship lead us into the Holy of Holies, but not without blood. The priests sprinkled the blood from the animal sacrifices on the Mercy Seat. Jesus is the Lamb who was slain, the sacrifice for our sins, and so unless you have accepted this, and received Him as your Saviour, no matter how much you pray or praise God, it will be *impossible* to enter His presence. Jesus is the *only* way. Worship begins with God. Because He first loved us, we can love Him. God gave instructions to Moses that the incense was to be made to a specific recipe, refined to be pure and holy.

> *'Beat some of it very fine and put some of it in front of the Ark of the Covenant, where I will meet with you in the Tabernacle. This incense is most holy. Never make this incense for yourselves. It is reserved for the Lord, and you must treat it as holy. Those who make it for their own enjoyment will be cut off from the community.'* Exodus 30:36–38. New Living Translation.

I emphasise again that it *has* to be done God's way. The altar faced the Ark of the Covenant, where the Lord promises to meet with us, *if* our worship and prayer is focused in that direction. The incense is most holy and must never be used for oneself. It is for God alone. It is set apart for God, to please *Him*, and is not to please you. Remind yourself of that the next time you are tempted to grumble that at your church the praise and worship or prayer is not in a style that you like. It only needs to please God, not you. When we worship, we are 'dying' to self, in other words, putting everything else aside, every distraction, every concern, every other desire, even our needs, and focusing on God alone. If you are focused on anything other than the Lord, you cannot enter the glory. Whom are you worshipping? God says, '*You shall have no other gods before me.*' Exodus 20:3. When you look upon Jesus, everything else disappears. We bring a sacrifice of praise to God and it is not something we do only when we feel like it or out of religious routine, but a sacrifice of our mind, our will and our emotions.

6

A Place To Meet With God

Beyond the Veil, to 'Life'

Immediately past the altar of incense is the curtain, leading into the Holy of Holies, or the 'Most Holy Place'.

> *"Make a curtain of blue, purple and scarlet yarn and finely twisted linen, with cherubim worked into it by a skilled craftsman ... Hang the curtain from the clasps and place the ark of the Testimony behind the curtain. The curtain will separate the Holy Place from the Most Holy Place."* Exodus 26: 31–33.

At the very moment when Jesus died on the cross, the curtain of the temple was torn in two from top to bottom. (see Matt. 27:51).

This curtain was forty-five feet high, fifteen feet wide and heavily embroidered, and yet at *that* moment it was torn from *top* to *bottom*. No human being could have done this. It had to be God tearing it from above. Suddenly the way was open into His presence. I often imagine this picture in my mind, of God at that very moment when Jesus gave up His Spirit on the cross, with tears in His eyes excitedly grabbing hold of that curtain, tearing it apart and shouting, "Yes! At last it's done, no longer do I have to have this barrier separating Me from My children. This is what I've been longing for!" The joy far outweighing the cost to Jesus.

> 'Therefore, brothers, since we have confidence to
> enter the Most Holy Place by the blood of Jesus, by a
> new and living way opened for us through the curtain,
> that is, his body, and since we have a great priest over
> the house of God, let us draw near to God with a
> sincere heart in full assurance of faith..'
> Heb.10: 19–22.

Jesus' body was that curtain painfully torn in two because of
love – God's love. Earlier, I said that in the Tabernacle we
have a foreshadowing of what was to come, a picture of all
that would be fulfilled in Jesus. It shows us how to come
into the presence of a perfectly holy and awesome God, who
loves us dearly and longs for us to come closer to Him.
Firstly, we enter in through the east gate into the Outer
Court. This gate is called 'the Way'. Here we are faced first
of all with the cross of Jesus.

> "If anyone would come after me, he must deny himself
> and take up his cross daily and follow me." Luke 9:23.

We are crucified with Christ, choosing to follow Him daily
and leave the past behind. The way to the presence of God,
the 'glory', is always via the cross, through repentance and
the waters of baptism, which is an outward sign of an
inward change, and daily cleansing of our sins.
The doorway into the Holy Place is called the 'Truth'
because it is here that we receive revelation of the truth
through the Word of God and the Spirit of God working
together. As this takes place, it causes us more and more to
come to God in praise, worship, intercession and thanks-

giving, drawing us in through the curtain, into the life of Jesus.

Jesus said, *"I am the way and the truth and the life. No-one comes to the Father except through me."* John 14:6. He is the *only* way to the throne of God and to the fullness of life in the plan He has for *you*. As we go through the curtain we enter into Life ... but what is this Life? Moses was instructed to have the curtain made of blue, purple and scarlet yarn and finely twisted linen, with cherubim worked into it. What are cherubim and why was this? Cherubim are not the little rosy-cheeked babies or toddlers often depicted on Christmas cards or in popular art. They are mighty angels, who stand in the presence of God and serve Him. In the book of Genesis, after Adam and Eve had sinned, they were driven out of the Garden of Eden.

'And the LORD God said, "The man has now become like one of us, knowing good and evil. He must not be allowed to reach out his hand and take also from the tree of life and eat, and live for ever." So the LORD God banished him from the Garden of Eden to work the ground from which he had been taken. After he drove the man out, he placed on the east side of the Garden of Eden cherubim and a flaming sword flashing back and forth to guard the way to the tree of life.' Gen. 3:22–24.

Adam and Eve had gone from total dependence and submission to God, where they were walking and talking with Him and living in His presence,- to independence and separation. From working in a beautiful and pleasant garden where there was peace and everything they needed, – to working hard ground that was cursed and full of thorns and thistles. Everlasting life, fullness of life, where we have everything we need in the presence of God, was found in the Garden of Eden, but man could not be allowed to retain it in his independent, unsubmitted state, and the entrance was guarded by cherubim and a flaming sword. The sword of God's judgment stood between man and life, and only through Jesus' death on the cross and payment of the penalty for our sin could we regain access. He is the way to true life.

The curtain was made of blue, purple and scarlet yarn and finely twisted white linen, and even this had meaning, showing that Jesus really is the way. Blue is the colour of the sky, which represents Jesus as the Son of God who came from heaven to earth, as He is portrayed in the gospel of John. Purple is the colour of royalty and sovereignty and was used to show that Jesus is king, as in Matthew's gospel. The blood that Jesus shed on the cross as the sacrifice for our sins was scarlet, and so scarlet was used in the curtain to symbolise Jesus as our Saviour, as He is depicted in the gospel of Luke. And the fine white linen represents Jesus as the perfect Man –the Son of Man as in the gospel of Mark. Every detail of the Tabernacle was significant, pointing to Jesus as the fulfilment. His body was the curtain that was torn in two to open the way to God. Everything is made complete in Him.

Our Father God longs for His children to be near Him. That was the whole reason He created us. He longs to wipe away our tears and to bless us. We don't need to worry about what we shall eat or drink or wear, or anything else.

> 'But seek first his kingdom and his righteousness, and all these things will be given to you as well.' Matt. 6:33.

Everything we need can be found in His presence, as is portrayed in the Holy of Holies. The first thing we come to in the Holy of Holies is the Ark of the Covenant, symbolising the presence of God among His people. Its presence on the battlefield was the guarantee of victory and its absence was believed to be the reason for defeat It represented God's covenant promises to His people, His contract. He would never leave them nor forsake them. He had chosen them and He would bring them into the Promised Land and to Himself.

> *"Have them make a chest of acacia wood – two and a half cubits long, a cubit and a half wide, and a cubit and a half high. Overlay it with pure gold, both inside and out, and make a gold moulding around it. Cast four gold rings for it and fasten them to its four feet, with two rings on one side and two rings on the other. Then make poles of acacia wood and overlay them with gold. Insert the poles into the rings on the sides of the chest to carry it … Then put into the ark the Testimony, which I will give you. Make an atonement cover of pure gold – two and a half cubits long and a cubit and a half wide. And make two cherubim out of hammered gold at the ends of the cover. Make one cherub on one end and the second cherub on the other."* Exodus 25:10–19.

The Ark was a simple wooden chest, covered with pure gold, both inside and out. I praise God that He takes the weak and the foolish things of this world and He raises them up to show His glory. We are but simple human beings, clay pots, as it were, who deserve nothing, and yet He chooses to clothe us in pure gold, the riches of Heaven. Clothed in

Christ, dressed in royal robes of righteousness that we surely don't deserve, we are heirs to the Kingdom of God. The Bible dictionary states that gold is used symbolically for the imperishable spiritual riches that God alone can give. His gifts are eternal. *'For He has clothed me with garments of salvation and arrayed me in a robe of righteousness.'* Isa. 61:10.

Into the simple vessel that was the Ark were placed the Tablets of stone with the Ten Commandments written on them.

> *"I will put my law in their minds and write it on their hearts."* Jer.31:33.

The Word of God is in us, as followers of Christ, and we have the mind of Christ.

According to Hebrews chapter 9, there was also placed in the Ark the golden jar that contained the manna, as a reminder of God's miraculous act in feeding His people in the wilderness. A sufficient amount was provided each day, showing us that when we are walking with Him, and following His ways, He will provide everything we need, as and when we need it. *'Give us this day our daily bread.'* Notice here also that the jar containing the manna was a *golden* jar, a rich provision. The Lord is not a mean God, but a God who loves us and wants to bless us richly.

Alongside the jar of manna was Aaron's staff that budded, symbolising that we are chosen as high priests (see Numbers 17) and are called to minister to the Lord beyond the curtain, at any time not just once a year, as in the Old Testament.

> *'But only the high priest entered the inner room, and that only once a year, and never without blood, which*

he offered for himself and for the sins the people had committed in ignorance. The Holy Spirit was showing by this that the way into the Most Holy Place had not yet been disclosed as long as the first tabernacle was still standing.' Heb.9:7–8.

Attached to the front of the turban worn by the priests in the tabernacle was a plaque of pure gold on which was engraved 'HOLY TO THE LORD.' As high priests, we are set apart for God's purposes through Jesus' death on the cross to make the way.

'But you are a chosen people, a royal priesthood, a holy nation, a people belonging to God.' 1 Peter 2:9.

'When Christ came as high priest of the good things that are already here, he went through the greater and more perfect tabernacle that is not man-made, that is to say, not part of this creation. He did not enter by means of the blood of goats and calves; but he entered the Most Holy Place once for all by his own blood, having obtained eternal redemption.' Heb. 9:11–12.

'For this reason Christ is the mediator of a new covenant, that those who are called may receive the promised eternal inheritance.' Heb. 9:15.

The cover of the ark (called the atonement cover) was made of pure gold with hammered gold cherubim at either end, all made of one piece, showing that they cannot be separated from the throne of God. The atonement cover was the place where God was said to dwell, the throne of God, and wherever the throne of

God is, there too are the guardian angels. *'The LORD is in his holy temple; the LORD is on his heavenly throne.'* Ps. 11:4.

It is the place where we are now able, because of what Jesus did, to approach with confidence and receive mercy and grace (see Heb. 4:16). Here we are made one with God.

The cherubim at either end of the cover had their wings spread upwards, overshadowing the throne, facing one another and looking towards the cover, symbolising that when we are seated with Christ in heavenly places, we are safe and have nothing to fear.

'He who dwells in the shelter of the Most High will rest in the shadow of the Almighty. I will say of the LORD, "He is my refuge and my fortress, my God in whom I trust." Surely he will save you from the fowler's snare and from the deadly pestilence. He will cover you with his feathers, and under his wings you will find refuge.' Ps. 91:1–4.

On our journey through the Tabernacle, first of all we see that there has to be a desire to know God and for the things of God, a heart cry to know Him, touch Him and see Him. Nothing is given by God unless there is a desire for it and no-one is ready for salvation or to go deeper unless they want it.

Next we step through the door called the 'Way', by believing that Jesus died on the cross for us, by turning away from our old lives in repentance and receiving Him by faith as our Lord and Saviour. We are born again and washed clean from our past sins by the blood of Jesus. Both salvation and the washing of our sins in repentance must become a daily practice if we want to move deeper into the fullness of God. We have been saved, are being saved and will continue to be saved, and must constantly keep short accounts with God, choosing His way rather than our own. Moving on, we enter into the 'Truth', where we 'eat' God's word in the light and power of the Holy Spirit, the Word and the Spirit working together as they have always done. You cannot have one without the other. God is waiting to reveal insight and revelation of truth to anyone who cares enough to search for it, but it is only as we start *living* the Word in the power and anointing of the Holy Spirit that it becomes a part of us. Just reading and studying the Word, or even receiving revelation, is not enough. We were given ten commandments, not ten suggestions, to act upon and live by, but there is no way that we can do it without the Holy Spirit's help. It is '*"not by might, nor by power, but by my Spirit,"* *says the Lord Almighty.'* He has put His law into our hearts.

This Christian walk is not all about what we can *get* for ourselves. It is about *giving*, giving our praise, thanks and worship to God and interceding for and giving to others at the altar of incense, focused on God *only.* Where is your attention directed when you are praising and worshipping? I asked the Lord once to really teach me how to worship Him in Spirit and truth, and His answer was, "It's not an experience, it's a lifestyle." You cannot come into your inheritance in Christ if you are a 'Sunday Christian'. Our praise and worship is a sweet aroma to God, and takes us through the curtain called 'Life', into "Eden life", fullness of life, where we have *all* that we need, our inheritance as sons of the King.

'To him who overcomes, I will give the right to sit with me on my throne, just as I overcame and sat down with my Father on his throne.' Rev. 3:21.

Jesus sat down because all His work was done. As the Father rested on the seventh day of creation because the work was finished, so Jesus rested, because the work was done. As we sit with Jesus on His throne, we are enveloped in the shekinah glory, the glory of heaven, which came and filled the Tabernacle, and we can be totally at peace, whatever our circumstances, resting in His arms, knowing that He is Lord over everything. We are protected under His wings; He feeds us and clothes us, and provides everything we need, just as He did for Adam. By His stripes we are healed and we are no longer captives to sin, but free. Everything, everything, everything comes from the presence of God, so it makes sense to seek first His Kingdom and His righteousness, so that everything else may be given to us as well. I do feel that I need to emphasise here that this is not a formula. It takes a broken and contrite heart, a heart that genuinely desires God's will above one's own. Revival comes out of brokenness, out of hearts turned back to God in submission and love, out of a love that puts Him first, before anything or anyone else. You need to love the Lord with all your heart, soul, mind and strength and to love others as yourself. And IT'S ALL A WORK OF HIS GRACE. We cannot *make* any of these things happen. All we can do is cry out to Him to work it in us, for even the desire for this does not originate from you but from Him, and then *you* take a step of faith. You do what you can and He will do what you can't. *'Seek first his kingdom and his righteousness ...'* What is a kingdom? It's the area where a king rules, so to seek first God's kingdom and His righteousness is to surrender *all* and to seek His will for every part of your life, with all your heart, soul, mind and strength, body and spirit, – the lot.

'Then the cloud covered the Tent of Meeting, and the glory of the LORD filled the tabernacle. Moses could not enter the Tent of Meeting because the cloud had settled upon it, and the glory of the LORD filled the tabernacle.' Ex.40:34–35.

Our sinful human life cannot enter the presence of God, so as we take this journey with Jesus, leaving the past behind, we will be filled with the wonderful glory of Heaven. The Tabernacle was built to contain the glory of God, which, as we have already discovered, is the goodness and presence of God in the form of Jesus. Now we can praise the Lord that His glory is no longer restricted to a small room or veiled by a curtain, but can be seen in every child of God who chooses to submit to Him. Jesus is the Way, the Truth and the Life; no-one comes to the Father except by Him, and no-one can see the glory of God except by Him. He *is* the King of Glory!

'For God who said, "Let light shine out of darkness," made his light shine in our hearts to give us the light of the knowledge of the glory of God in the face of Christ. But we have this treasure in jars of clay to show that this all-surpassing power is from God and not from us. We are hard pressed on every side, but not crushed; perplexed, but not in despair; persecuted, but not abandoned; struck down but not destroyed. We always carry around in our body the death of Jesus, so that the life of Jesus may also be revealed in our body.' 2 Cor.4:6–10.

7

Four Visions From God

The First Vision

The Rock on which we Stand.

My eyes were closed and my hands held up to the heavens as we worshipped the Lord in church that morning. Suddenly, without even realising it, I stopped singing, lost in the wonder and the presence of my God. No longer was I in the church with a thousand other people, but I stood alone at the foot of a huge mountain. As I was standing there, my eyes were drawn up, and to my surprise, the mountain changed and became Jesus. What started as the rocky surface changed to become the folds of His robe. His hands were stretched up towards heaven and yet at the same time reached out over the earth, and there was lightning coming from His fingertips, like huge fireworks lighting up the sky. I looked towards His face, but there was a cloud covering it, blocking it from view, and yet, as can only happen in a dream or vision, I could see that His hair was pure white. He appeared to be much, much older than the Jesus who came to earth as a man, but even though I couldn't see His face, I *knew* it was Him. And He was *so* big: a huge mountain and a huge Jesus, a truly awesome and magnificent sight.

Later, as I pondered on the vision, wondering what it meant and what the Lord was saying to me, the Holy Spirit prompted me to look in the Bible to see what each detail of the vision signified. It's funny, whenever I've received visions from the Lord, even though they are amazing, they often seem almost 'matter of fact' at the time and it's not until later as I look at them more closely to see what the Lord is saying that I become *really* excited.The mountain that I saw was the 'Mountain of the Lord', the 'Holy Mountain' where God's presence is, and as we've already discovered, if His presence is there, then so also is His goodness, and the 'goodness' of God is Jesus. So it's on the mountain of God, in His presence, that we *see* Jesus. The sixth chapter of Isaiah describes the occasion when he was in the presence of God and saw the Lord, and John 12:41 confirms that it was Jesus whom he beheld. It was on the mountain of Sinai that Moses received the Ten Commandments, spoken by God, and, allegorically speaking, it is on the mountain of God that we receive revelation and understanding of His Word, and the source of our Christian growth. The Scripture speaks of the Lord's temple being established in the hearts of His people.

'In the last days the mountain of the LORD'S temple will be established as chief among the mountains; it will be raised above the hills, and all nations will stream to it. Many peoples will come and say, "Come, let us go up to the mountain of the LORD, to the house of the God of Jacob. He will teach us his ways, so that we may walk in his paths."' Isaiah 2:2–3.

This mountain also represents the rock of Jesus, the foundation stone on which the house of God is built. The wise man builds his house on that rock. (See Matt. 7:24–27)

'Trust in the LORD forever, for the LORD, the LORD is the Rock eternal.' Isaiah 26:4. The children of Israel *'... drank from the spiritual rock that accompanied them, and that rock was Christ.'* 1 Cor.10:4.

He is our strength to stand in a fallen world. The Psalmist speaks of the rock as being our salvation, our redeemer and our fortress.In my vision, there was lightning coming from Jesus' fingertips, depicting the awesome power and majesty of God, as in the manifestation of God's presence on Mount Sinai recorded in Exodus 19.

In Psalm 77:18, we read, *'Your thunder was heard in the whirlwind, your lightning lit up the world; the earth trembled and quaked,'* and in Psalm 18:12, *'Out of the brightness of his presence clouds advanced, with hailstones and bolts of lightning.'* In Revelation 4:15, John describes his vision of the Throne of Heaven, *'From the throne came flashes of lightning, rumblings and peals of thunder.'* In the notes of the NIV Study Bible, we are told that, 'In Revelation, thunder and lightning always mark an important event connected with the heavenly temple.' So presumably, this vision was to tell me something important connected with this, although the understanding of it came to me more as I received the rest of the series of visions.

'Then the cloud covered the Tent of Meeting, and the glory of the LORD filled the tabernacle.' Ex. 40:34.

The cloud covered or veiled the glory of God because its brightness was more than the children of Israel could bear, and this explains why, in my vision, there was a cloud covering His face. The glory of God is found in the face of Jesus and its brightness is more than we can stand in our human bodies.

'"But," he said, "you cannot see my face, for no-one may see me and live."' Ex. 33:20.

In Revelation chapter one, John's revelation of Jesus Christ, he sees one *'like a son of man'*, the Lord Jesus. *'His head and hair were white like wool, as white as snow.'* And in Daniel 7:9, in his vision, Daniel saw the *'Ancient of Days'* (God the Father), also with white hair. When we have seen the Son, we have seen the Father. *'The Alpha and the Omega, who is, and who was, and who is to come, the Almighty.'* Rev. 1:8. Jesus *is* the wisdom of God, as depicted by His white hair. He is the One who died and rose again to make the way for us to Life. *'When I (John) saw him (Jesus), I fell at his feet as though dead. Then he placed his right hand on me and said: "Do not be afraid. I am the First and the Last. I am the Living One; I was dead, and behold I am alive forever and ever! And I hold the keys of death and Hades."'* Rev. 1.17–18. Jesus said, *"I AM* the First and the Last … the Living One." Jesus is the way to God, because He *is* God. John was familiar with Jesus, for he knew Him and had lived with Him and yet here, John really *saw* Jesus as He now is and was overwhelmed with His majesty.In the same way, we too need a revelation of *who* Jesus really is. In Matthew 16:13–19, Jesus asked His disciples,

'"Who do people say the Son of Man is?" They replied, "Some say John the Baptist; others say Elijah; and still others, Jeremiah or one of the prophets." "But what about you?" he asked. "Who do you say I am?" Simon Peter answered, "You are the Christ, the Son of the living God." Jesus replied, "Blessed are you, Simon son of Jonah, for this was not revealed to you by man, but by my Father in heaven. And I tell you that you are Peter, and on this rock I will

build my church, and the gates of Hades will not over-
come it. I will give you the keys of the kingdom of
heaven."

'Simon Peter *saw* Jesus, had a revelation of *who* Jesus is and
confessed it. On *that* revelation, the church will be built up,
as *God* wants it built. And on that same revelation, the way
is unlocked to fullness of life and the glory of God, even in
our time on this earth. Who is Jesus to you? In my vision I
saw a *big* Jesus. How big is your God? This can only be
shown to you by our Father in Heaven and not by man, so
the *only* way to receive this revelation and the key to the
kingdom life is by seeking Him through Jesus, in the power
of the Holy Spirit, and *not* by following religion.

There have been a number of occasions over the years
when I have been present at 'religious' meetings. One
instance was in a High Anglican church, where the people
were praying for the dead and blankly reading prayers from
a book. Another time was when different denominations had
met together and were trying to please one another.
Sometimes, I have even been in very charismatic meetings
where everyone *appeared* to be free but had slipped into a
routine of 'that's the way we do it'. On each of these occasions, there was such a sense of heaviness, sadness and
emptiness that I found myself sobbing uncontrollably,
without knowing why. I felt a pain that was almost physical,
which hurt so much that I wanted to leave, and once or twice
I did leave. What I was sensing was the grief of the Holy
Spirit at this cold manmade religion. God hates religion.
That's why He made a way for us to have a heart relationship
with Him through Jesus. Most of these people, bless them,
either didn't understand or had slipped into a routine. They
needed a life-transforming encounter with the Lord.

My first vision was wonderful, but I later realised that if we are standing at the bottom of the mountain looking up, then we are looking from a distance. It's like Old Testament religion with rules and regulations but no personal relationship with the Lord. The children of Israel could only look from a distance, and when the Tabernacle was built, could only enter the Outer Court and go no further. Many times they complained that they were better off in Egypt and wanted to go back, even though they had actually come out of poverty and hardship. Moses came out of wealth and yet never once wanted to go back. The difference was that Moses had experienced a 'burning bush' encounter with God, and the people had not. This vision is like being in the Outer Court of the Temple, or even looking through the doorway. You may know a little about God, having heard or read about Him, you may be going to church, and even praying because you see that Jesus is the right way, but there's no real life there, no personal relationship. It's religion, simply going through the motions of being a Christian.

> *'"Not everyone who says to me, 'Lord, Lord,' will enter the kingdom of heaven, but only he who does the will of my Father who is in heaven. Many will say to me on that day, 'Lord, Lord, did we not prophesy in your name, and in your name drive out demons and perform many miracles?' Then I will tell them plainly,' I never knew you. Away from me, you evil doers!"'*
> Matthew 7:21–23.

These are believers who have not received a revelation of who Jesus *really* is. The *will of the Father* is to come *through* the gate called the 'Way', laying down your life on the altar and being washed clean of all your sins. Perhaps you've done that, been born again and baptised, but you've gone no further, either because you didn't know and thought that was all, or because you were afraid through lack of understanding , like the people in the doctor's waiting room (see chapter two). There is no power in your Christian walk. You are looking at Jesus and His glory from a distance, from the bottom of the mountain, as it were.'For all have sinned and fall short of the glory of God.' We are missing out on His best for us, He has something far better for us and so He's calling us to go higher and deeper to receive it. He is able to do immeasurably more than all we could ask or imagine.Seeing Jesus and having revelation that He is the Son of God who died on the cross for you, to pay the price for your sin, washing you clean to make the way for you to approach the Father, is the first foundation in the building of God's Temple in your life. The solid rock on which you must now build is Jesus, our rock and our salvation.

8

Four Visions From God

The Second Vision

Come up Higher

Some weeks later, once again lost in worship in the presence of God, I had a second vision. As in my first vision, I stood at the base of a huge mountain and as my eyes were drawn upwards, the mountain became Jesus. But this time, He bent down towards me and, giving me His full attention, He stretched out His hand saying, "Come up higher, come closer." I started to climb, His outstretched hand constantly drawing me nearer, right into the arms of Jesus. As those big arms held me close, I was filled with an overwhelming sense of His love, and in this place I felt safe and protected. I could hear His heartbeat and I could gaze upon His wonderful face. From here I could see what He could see. I could even feel His very breath on my cheek. I was so close, and I could hear that still small voice. Best of all, I could wrap my arms around His neck and kiss Him, like a small child loving his or her father. It felt so good, as though I'd come home. I was where I belonged.

'The Lord descended to the top of Mount Sinai and called Moses to the top of the mountain.' Exodus 19:20.

This was a place where they could talk to each other face to face. We think that we are reaching out to God, when in actual fact, He is reaching out to us. He doesn't want us standing in the Outer Court looking from a distance. He's reaching out to you now and saying, "Come up higher, come closer, I want to talk with you. I want to wipe away your tears and take away your pain. Don't be afraid, just trust Me. I have a wonderful plan and purpose for your life." We have a choice to make; do we want to go higher? Climbing a mountain takes effort, commitment and desire. What you cannot manage on your own, God will enable you to do, but *you* have to make the choice. Aaron had been invited by God to go up the mountain with Moses (Exodus 19:24), but he never went. Why not? Because he feared man more than he feared God, and he chose to please man in preference to God.

When I was at YWAM in 1994 for a Discipleship Training School, the outreach at the end of the course was an eight week visit to Uganda. This was not compulsory, but we were encouraged to go and so were given a short period of time to make up our minds. I was *so* afraid. What could I do in Uganda? I'd never done any real preaching or teaching. I wasn't a nurse, I wasn't gifted in children's work. What would it be like there? Would I cope with the culture and environment? I was a window dresser, for goodness' sake, and there wasn't a lot of call for that in Uganda. So I prayed, almost hoping that God would say, "No, it's OK Rose, I have something much easier for you to do," but of course He didn't. In fact I heard nothing. Over and over I asked, "Lord, if You want me to go, I will, but you'll have to tell me. Do you want me to go?" Still I heard nothing. Eventually, I had to make a decision. I'd come this far, and I couldn't go back now, so even though I was petrified, I would go to Uganda. I *had* to go. Once I had made the decision, I felt a total peace come over me and I realised that the decision the Lord had wanted me to make was this: would I step out in faith, choosing to trust Him, or would I choose to play safe and do nothing? That decision not only changed my life, but also, in time, affected many other lives. We have a lifetime of choices to make, whether to go on, climbing higher and drawing nearer even when it's hard and we're afraid, or whether to stay safe, watching from a distance, saying it's because we haven't heard from God, waiting for Him to do it all. No, the Lord says, "*You* make the decision. What do *you* want? You take the first step, and then I will take you by the hand and lead you all the way. Do you fear God or man?"

'He tends his flock like a shepherd: he gathers the lambs in his arms and carries them close to his heart.'
Isaiah 40:11.

"How do you see Heaven?" That is a question once put to us in our church, one which stopped me in my tracks. It was something I'd never thought about before, so I asked, "Lord, how *do* I see Heaven?" Immediately I had a picture of myself as a small child in my father's arms, that is, in the arms of Jesus, and I thought, "That's right, that *is* how I see Heaven." When small children are in the arms of their parents, they feel safe, held tight and secure in their parents' love. It's a place where children can be in total peace and want for nothing. When you are living in the arms of Jesus, nothing can harm you.

In His arms, we are so close that we become as one with Him, hearing His heartbeat, so that we can know His heart for us in every situation. In Jesus' arms, His face is no longer completely hidden by a cloud. We can see Him more clearly, even though only as a poor reflection in a mirror, but what we fix our eyes on we will reflect, so we will become more like Him. *'And we, who with unveiled faces all reflect the Lord's glory, are being transformed into His likeness with ever increasing glory, which comes from the Lord.'* 2 Cor. 3:18. If a person constantly looks at evil and anger, that's what he will reflect, and in the same way, if we are constantly looking at the love of God in the face of Jesus, through His Word, that is what we will reflect. We will begin to see others and ourselves as He sees us instead of as the world sees us or as circumstances dictate.His breath is the breath of God that was breathed into Adam's nostrils, bringing life, the Holy Spirit that Jesus breathed on His disciples saying, *"Receive the Holy Spirit."* John 20:22. It is as though we are held tightly in His arms, in this intimate place, immersed in Him, baptised in His Holy Spirit. We hear that still small voice, His gentle whisper, speaking tenderly of His love for us, causing us to love Him in return. It is as though we can kiss Him, which is to worship Him.

This second vision is a picture of coming into the Holy of Holies, right into the presence of God, into a new intimacy. He's drawn us closer, into a deeper commitment, after passing through the Holy Place. We've climbed the mountain through the baptism of the Holy Spirit, so that now we can pray in the Spirit, and we've spent time learning to know Him through His Word. The Word and the Spirit work together, as in the Holy Place. It is only when you have seen Him and have become this close that you can truly worship Him. Your focus is totally on Him and so you leave all your problems and your past behind. You cannot take a backpack or a corpse up the mountain with you, as they would weigh you down and prevent you from climbing.

"You shall have no other gods before me," says the Lord. *'For He chose us in him before the creation of the world to be holy and blameless in his sight. In love he predestined us to be adopted as his sons through Jesus Christ, in accordance with his purpose and will.'* Eph. 1:4–5.

God had a plan for your life even before the world was made, and His plan was that you would be set apart for Him. He chose you, *wanted* you to be His child. He loves us so much that He sent Jesus to die for us to make the way.

'In him we were also chosen, having been predestined according to the plan of him who works out everything in conformity with the purpose of his will, in order that we who were the first to hope in Christ, might be for the praise of his glory. And you also were included in Christ when you heard the word of truth, the gospel of your salvation. Having believed, you were marked in him with a seal, the promised Holy Spirit.' Eph. 1:11–13.

It was only when you really heard the word of truth, really saw Jesus and were given a revelation of Him, that you received this truth and accepted it, but you had to choose it. Having believed and chosen, you then received the Holy Spirit to seal the relationship and to enable you by His power to live as a child of God. Although this is God's plan and desire, He will not force us into anything. He wants us to *choose* to love Him, to choose His way, and then He will enable us to do His will. When we have children, we want them to love us, but no matter how much we love and care for them, we cannot force them to return that love. The choice is theirs, as the choice is ours whether to love God and accept His way or not.

'But because of His great love for us, God, who is rich in mercy, made us alive with Christ even when we were dead in transgressions – it is by grace you have been saved. And God raised us up with Christ and seated us with him in the heavenly realms in Christ Jesus.' Eph. 2:4–6.

Even when we were at our most rebellious, Jesus came to show us the way to the fullness of the life God originally planned for us.

'For the Son of Man came to seek and save what was lost.' Luke 19:10.

When we choose to go with Him and to believe what He has done, we can *see* that He has already seated us with our loving Father in Christ Jesus. We are in the heavenly realms in the presence and goodness of God, in His glory.

'But now in Christ Jesus you who once were far away have been brought near through the blood of Christ.' Eph. 2:13

The second foundation to the building of the temple of God is a realisation of who you are in Christ, that He lives in you by His Holy Spirit and you live in Him. This is the place in which we were created to be, and so when we come to the understanding of that, it's like coming home. We are made one with Jesus.

9

Four Visions From God

The Third Vision: The Throne Room

*'One thing I ask of the LORD, this is what I seek: that
I may dwell in the house of the LORD all the days of
my life, to gaze upon the beauty of the LORD and to
seek him in his temple.'* Ps. 27:4.

There is no place I'd rather be than in the presence of my
God, standing before His throne, or sitting at His feet. One
real glimpse of His beautiful face and you will never be the
same. I'm in love with Jesus.

That's how I felt that day, as I was again lost in worship. I
stepped boldly through the veil into the Most Holy Place
and as I worshipped, like Isaiah, I saw the Lord seated on
His throne. He was raised up high in this vision, and the
beautiful rich fabric of His robe flowed, like water, down the
long steps that led to His throne. I stopped, unable to go any
further, full of wonder at being so close yet almost wanting
to turn and run because it was so awesome. All I could see
was Jesus as He stood and walked towards me. A smile was
on His face, and He looked so pleased to welcome me. As I
stood there, He put a royal robe around my shoulders, made
of beautiful rich velvet embroidered with gold and edged in
an ocelot type of fur, which trailed on the floor as I walked.
Then He put a magnificent crown on my head and held out

a golden sceptre to me, which I took, but then put back into His hands. In this vision, Jesus was seated on His throne and raised up. I had to look up to Him. I saw Him as a King on His throne, the *Lord* over all, and yet his robe, His glory and goodness, His love flowed like a river, down from the throne to me. Too often we reduce Jesus to a size we can handle, an image that *we* have created. Yes, Jesus is our friend, God is a loving Father, but He is also the Judge of all and a consuming fire. He is the King of kings and Creator of the heavens and the earth. God is a holy God and must be held in reverence.

> *"Among those who approach me I will show myself holy; in the sight of all the people I will be honoured."*
> Lev. 10:3.

Sometimes it is as if He calls us into His arms for a cuddle, but at other times the sight is so awesome that we dare not move, and yet His goodness still flows out to us.

In Zechariah's fourth vision, the Angel of the Lord says to Joshua,

> *"See, I have taken away your sin, and I will put rich garments on you."* Zec. 3:4.

The robe of righteousness signifies that we are made right with God. Joshua had been accused as a criminal, but then justified. He had been dressed in filthy, polluted clothes, but these were replaced with rich garments. By the grace of God, through what Jesus did on the cross, our sins are taken away, we are totally forgiven, and He enables us to leave our old self behind. As I came before Jesus in the vision, He put a royal robe around my shoulders. He clothed me in

Himself, and I am covered by His blood. *Royal robes* declare that I am a son of the King, an heir with Jesus to the Kingdom of God. I can claim my inheritance of everything that the Bible says is mine: acceptance, favour, strength, healing, prosperity, joy and peace. And best of all, I inherit the character of Jesus.

> *"The Spirit of the Lord is on me, because he has anointed me to preach good news to the poor. He has sent me to proclaim freedom for the prisoners and recovery of sight for the blind, to release the oppressed, to proclaim the year of the Lord's favour."* Luke 4:18–19.

The words spoken by Jesus in the synagogue, after He had been baptised in the River Jordan and filled with the Holy Spirit, tell why He had come. The royal robe that was put upon me represents that we have been given the same Spirit as Jesus. In 2 Kings, Elisha received the mantle of Elijah. He had asked for a double portion of Elijah's spirit and was enabled to perform double the miracles. Jesus said,

> *"I tell you the truth, anyone who has faith in me will do what I have been doing. He will do even greater things than these, because I am going to the Father."* John 14:12.

The Spirit of the Sovereign Lord is upon *you* and is *in* you. If you have received Jesus as your Saviour, God the Father has anointed you to do even greater things than Jesus did, in *His* name and in *His* power. *You* have inherited His mantle, as it were.

The Lord placed a crown on my head. This represents the

crown of life, everlasting life and fullness of life, as promised to those who have stood the test and love God (see James 1:12). It's the crown of glory – God's goodness that will never fade away (see 1Peter 5:4). And it's the crown of love and compassion (see Psalm 103:4).On the day of my wedding, the Lord demonstrated this to me. Due to various reasons, at the last minute, I had no headdress in which to be married. A friend offered to loan me hers, but on the very day, I was *given* the most beautiful tiara in the bridal shop. God had already *given* me the wedding dress, as previously promised in a vision, and now He had put a crown upon my head, as if to crown my new life with Gerry. You cannot borrow your Christianity from anyone else or inherit it from your parents. It's a personal thing. The crown of life comes directly from God to you as a gift. It's a personal, intimate relationship between you and the Lord that is to last forever. He gave me a beautiful wedding dress. He clothed me in white, symbolising that I was washed clean and made pure. A crown was placed upon my head, the crown of life, and sapphires and diamonds, precious stones, were placed around my neck. We are sons and daughters of the King, and His desire is to bless us richly.

'And you also were included in Christ when you heard the word of truth, the gospel of your salvation. Having believed, you were marked in him with a seal, the promised Holy Spirit, who is a deposit guaranteeing our inheritance until the redemption of those who are God's possession—to the praise of his glory.' Eph. 1:13–14

The sceptre is the rod of a ruler, symbolising his power. When the king extends the sceptre, he offers entrance and favour. It represents his power and authority. In the book of Esther, when she touches the tip of the king's sceptre, she is acknowledging her acceptance of his grace, without which she knows that she would surely have been put to death. In my vision, not only did I touch the sceptre, I also took it from the Lord. By doing this, I was accepting not only His grace but also the power and authority that the King of kings alone can give. I then put the sceptre back into His hands as an act of submission, realising that to have authority we must come under authority. The gifts that God gives to us are to be used for *His* glory and the furthering of *His* Kingdom and not for our own purposes. He gives us authority to trample on snakes and scorpions and over all the power of the enemy, but this is not to make us look good. It is to glorify *Him*. It is easy for us to become proud and start to worship the gift instead of the Giver. When this happens, even though the gift was given to us by God, it becomes an idol and is our enemy. God is a jealous God. He will not share us, and because He loves us, He will crush our enemies. When this happens, it hurts. What God gives to us *must* be surrendered back to Him.

In the first vision, I saw a big Jesus, the rock, and I saw the need for a relationship rather than a religion. I realised that it was like being in the Outer Court of the Temple and seeing from a distance. I came through the gate called the 'Way', was confronted with the cross and was born again. In the second vision, I came through into the Truth, into the Holy Place. I drew nearer by climbing the mountain, through reading God's Word, listening to His Holy Spirit and receiving the baptism of the Holy Spirit. The relationship grew as I drew closer and I climbed right into the arms of Jesus where I fell in love with Him. I believe that we can only truly worship the Lord in Spirit and truth when we've been in this place. When I climbed into His arms, I had to leave all problems and my past (the corpse) behind. I learned of my position in Christ, seated with Him in heavenly places. Following on, in this third vision I saw a holy God, a powerful King, and discovered and received my inheritance, which can *only* come from drawing near to God in the Holy of Holies. Everything is in there, in that intimate place with Jesus. In the Holiest Place we find the answers to our prayers and everything we need, provision, acceptance, intimacy, salvation, protection, direction, forgiveness and healing. All the promises of God can be received in His presence.

'Seek first his kingdom and his righteousness and all these things will be given to you as well.' Matt. 6:33.

In finding out about my inheritance, I find out what is mine and so am equipped with everything I need, that is, anointing, love, compassion, power and authority. I have now entered the 'Life'. We must remember that we have to seek Him first for who He is, and not for what He will give us. Our relationship *must* come first. Adam had a relationship with God before Eve was created, and it's the same for us today. Before you can receive your inheritance and the best that God has for you, including a husband or wife, your relationship with Him must be the first priority.

10

Four Visions From God

The Fourth Vision: The Great Commission

What more could we want? We're saved, filled with the Holy Spirit, we know who we are and what we have inherited and we've had some wonderful experiences with God in worship. My friend, it's not about what *we* want, it's about what *God* wants. We have been bought with a price. We no longer belong to ourselves. There is more ... true freedom and fulfilment come from being submitted to *His* will for our lives. He has wonderful things in store for us, which are exciting but which will also challenge us. Only those who overcome will be given the right to eat from the tree of life. This brings me to my fourth vision.I was back at the mountain again, but this time I didn't wait to be called, I *wanted* to climb up there quickly. I fixed my eyes on Jesus and started boldly on the journey, knowing that I was welcome any time. It wasn't an easy climb, because the way was steep and some of the rocks were sharp and difficult to hold. Sometimes I was tempted to look back, but whenever I tried, I slipped. When I took my focus away from Jesus and worried about the difficult climb, I became afraid and tempted to give up, but when I looked to Him the climb seemed easier and I was able to continue. Eventually I reached the very peak of the mountain, where I stood with Jesus; the climb had been worth the effort. I was holding on tightly with one arm linked through His and we were waving our other arms in the air as though cheering and celebrating, having a wonderful time. A strong wind was blowing our clothes and hair, but I wasn't afraid because He was with me and I realised that He was holding on to me more securely than I was holding on to Him. A sense of total joy and peace overwhelmed me. I looked down through the clouds and saw the nations of the world, and in every direction I turned, I saw the waves of the sea lapping on the different shorelines. I saw fields and roads, trees and houses. God's creation truly was a wonderful sight.As we looked, Jesus said, "I will give you the nations." Then He went on to say, "In the beginning, God said, 'Let there be light' and there was light. Now you do the same." So in this time of worship, back in the church in Horsham, I reached out my hand as a prophetic gesture and spoke out God's light over the nations.

When you go mountain climbing, it is necessary to move each arm and leg alternately, letting go of each point of security. You cannot go higher or further unless you let go of what you were holding on to. In the same way, as a child of God, if you try to hold on to your past and the things you've known before, you cannot go higher. Carrying a backpack with a corpse in it will weigh you down. If your security and identity are in your own strength, your marriage partner, your job, your children or parents or even your ministry, it will hinder you from going on. Submit everything to the Lord. When Abraham offered his beloved son Isaac as a sacrifice in obedience to God, he was surrendering everything, his hopes, dreams and even the promises that God had given Him. He did it because he feared God and knew that in spite of what seemed to be, He was faithful and sovereign over all.

*"Now I know that you fear God, because you have not
withheld from me your son, your only son."*
Gen. 22:12.

Sometimes in our Christian walk we go through phases
when it seems as if all our props are removed, and everything that we've known and relied on and are familiar with
is no longer there. One such occasion for me was on that
first trip to Uganda with YWAM. I'd had quite a culture
shock and wasn't finding the trip easy. I was in a strange
country, where I didn't speak the language. I'd left my
home and business. My daughter had grown up and didn't
need me any more, or so it felt. I didn't know what the
future held, or where I would go, and I'd used up all my
money to pay for the Discipleship Training course. I felt
lost, empty and vulnerable as though I had nothing left.
My identity had been in my work, my home, my ministry
as a worship leader and being a mother to Keeli, and
suddenly, all that was gone. This is how my conversation
went with the Lord: "Lord, who am I?" I asked. "You are
the love of God," He replied. "How can I be the love of
God?" I questioned Him, confused, and He explained,
"You are an expression of the love of God. You are a gift
from God and a gift to God and you are a gift to others. It's
the same gift inside each person who belongs to Me, but
the wrappings are different. Some are black and some are
white." God wants us to lean on Him and realise that we
belong to Him, we are not our own. He wants us to be free
so that He can use us as a channel for His glory and
purposes. It's the whole person who climbs the mountain.
First, the Holy Spirit in us gives us the desire in our spirit,
then we make the decision with our mind, which is the
soul, and then our body puts in the physical effort. The

more we submit to God and focus on Him, the easier the journey will be.

Standing on the peak of the mountain, holding on to Jesus, means that you are exposed and vulnerable.

> *"You are the light of the world. A city on a hill cannot be hidden. Neither do people light a lamp and put it under a bowl. Instead they put it on its stand, and it gives light to everyone in the house. In the same way, let your light shine before men, that they may see your good deeds and praise your Father in heaven."* Matt.5:14–16.

> The Message Bible expresses it like this: *"You're here to be a light, bringing out the God-colours in the world. God is not a secret to be kept. We're going public with this, as public as a city on a hill. If I make you light-bearers, you don't think I'm going to hide you under a bucket, do you? I'm putting you on a light stand. Now that I've put you there on a hilltop, on a light stand – shine! Keep open house; be generous with your lives. By opening up to others, you'll prompt people to open up with God, this generous Father in Heaven.*

You are exposed to the world, people are watching you. What do they see and hear? Do they see God's hand on you, as you trust Him, even in a storm? One thing is certain, He is holding on to you much more than you are holding on to Him and He will never let go of your hand. Child of God, believe it and you will see.

I looked *through* the clouds over the nations. Earlier, in my second vision, when I was in the arms of Jesus, I was in the cloud of glory *with* Him, seeing the world through God's perspective and feeling His heartbeat. His creation truly *is* beautiful, and as you look at it through His eyes, you will begin to see more and more how intricate and awesome it is, but you will also see the effects of the enemy's hand leaving a trail of destruction. There are many needs out there, many hurting people who need a Saviour.

"Open your eyes and look at the fields! They are ripe for harvest." John 4:35.

Take a good look, my friend, because *you* have the answer within you. Jesus said to me, "I will give you the nations." It's God's will that none should perish, but that everyone should come to a saving knowledge of Him through Jesus, '… *that at the name of Jesus every knee should bow, in heaven and on earth and under the earth, and every tongue confess that Jesus Christ is Lord, to the glory of God the Father.'* Phil. 2:10–11.

God's word to the coming Saviour in Psalm 2:8 was, '*Ask of me, and I will make the nations your inheritance, the ends of the earth your possession.'*

John 17 tells how Jesus *did* ask this, when He prayed for His disciples, both present and future, that they might be one, one with each other and one with God the Father through Jesus, so that the world would know His love and glory. And then in Matthew 28:18–20, Jesus gave this commission to His disciples:

"All authority in heaven and on earth has been given to me. Therefore go and make disciples of all nations,

baptising them in the name of the Father and of the Son and of the Holy Spirit, and teaching them to obey everything I have commanded you. And surely I am with you always, to the very end of the age." "And these signs will accompany those who believe: In my name they will drive out demons; they will speak in new tongues; they will pick up snakes with their hands; and when they drink deadly poison, it will not hurt them at all; they will place their hands on sick people, and they will get well." Mark 16:17–18.

These signs *will* accompany those who believe; not *might* but *will* accompany them, *all* those who believe; not only some of the leaders, but *all believers*. God is the same yesterday, today and forever, so these signs were not just for those times. Ask yourself, "Do I really believe?" If the answer is no, ask the Lord for His help and then step out and do it. The only way to do it is to do it. God is bigger than your mistakes. Choose to believe what His Word says and remind yourself of it regularly. Declare the truth of God's Word over yourself: The Bible is full of positive truths.

'He that is in me is greater than he that is in the world.' ~ 'With God all things are possible.' ~ 'It is not by might, nor by power, but by my Spirit, says the Lord.' ~ 'Beloved, I desire above all things that you should prosper and be in health.'

In the beginning, when God said, "Let there be light," and there *was* light, He *spoke* it into being. You can do the same. Speak the light of life, life in all its fullness, as it was originally created to be. God's words are creative, even when spoken by *you*.

'For with you is the fountain of life; in your light we see light.' Psalm 36:9.

In other words, in God's presence there is revelation. In His presence we see the truth, the revelation to live the life that His Word says He has given to us. *Only* as you receive revelation that you *have* received this life can you let your light shine before men and be an imitator of God, and *only* in His presence can you receive revelation. Isaiah saw the Lord, but as he drew closer, he saw that he was a man of unclean lips who lived among a people of unclean lips. The closer we draw to the Lord, the more we see how unworthy we are, how much dirt there is on ourselves and in the world.

'Then one of the seraphs flew to me with a live coal in his hand, which he had taken with tongs from the altar. With it he touched my mouth and said, "See, this has touched your lips; your guilt is taken away and your sin atoned for." Then I heard the voice of the Lord saying, "Whom shall I send? And who will go for us?"' Isaiah 6:6–8.

It is a mark of spiritual maturity, when you see your own helplessness and realise how little you know, to acknowledge that it has to be Him. No matter what you think of yourself, God *has* chosen you and *nothing* is impossible for Him *if* you surrender your life to Him. If you are willing, He is more than able to fulfil His purpose for you. My fourth vision depicts our commission to go and give out what we've received, and where we live the life of Jesus. What God has given to you is for you to pass on to others and you will see signs and wonders following you. The message of all four visions is clear. There are four stages of your growing relationship with Jesus: the bride getting to know her husband: the maiden getting to know her King: understanding what our inheritance is in Christ: and acknowledging our responsibility to spread the Gospel. New birth is an event, but spiritual growth is a process, with no shortcuts, a process that we have to go through if we are to grow and move into the fullness of life and the plan that God has for us. Please note again that this is a process and NOT a formula. There are no formulae in our relationship with God and the journey will vary immensely for each of us. God can and will use us powerfully at any stage of the journey He chooses – if we are willing.In the first vision, I was confronted with Jesus and that He is alive and real. He is the Way into the presence of God and the rock on which I must build my relationship with the Father. Confrontation with what He has done by dying on the cross to take away the sin that separates us from our Father is the first foundation to building our spiritual temples which God wants to fill with His glory.

The second vision showed me that God wants us to have a oneness with Him through Jesus. As a bride is made one with her husband, so we are to be one with Jesus in a close intimate relationship. We are *in* Him and He is *in* us and God is our Father. The second foundation of our spiritual temple, built on the rock of Jesus, is to know and believe where we are seated and where we belong – in Christ Jesus. In this vision, using the analogy of the tabernacle, it was like coming from the Outer Court, through the Holy Place of learning and experiencing the power of the Holy Spirit, right into the Holy of Holies, where the presence of God is found.

The third vision represents the third foundation, our inheritance in Christ. We are heirs, with Christ, to the

Kingdom of God and the riches of Heaven, to the authority of Jesus and the anointing of the Holy Spirit. Provision and healing, in fact everything that the Bible says is ours, belong to us even in this life. In the throne room is the place where we find the answer to our prayers. It is the place of receiving but also the place of giving to God the glory and honour and praise that He deserves. Everything has been given to us by grace. We cannot earn it, only believe and receive it, and we can only believe if we know what there is to receive. The very moment that we were born again, we became sons of God and inherited all this, but it is only by faith that we can take hold of it. We can worship the Lord simply for who He is and not for what we can get, which would be pointless when He's already given it to us. Don't try to get what you already have.

Then we come to the fourth vision – the commission to go; to make disciples of all nations. This is how you actually live the life of Jesus. Freely you have received, now freely give. God wants His power released so that His glory will be seen in all the earth. This is the place of full surrender, where we lay aside what we want for what God wants. Revival comes when people are broken of self and see their need of God, realising that they cannot do anything worthwhile in their own strength and allowing His love to flow freely through them to others.

Look around you. The world is in a mess and people are crying out not knowing which way to turn. They say, "If there is a God, where is He? Why doesn't He do something?" God *has* done something. He did it two thousand years ago when Jesus came. Yes, there *is* a God and His Holy Spirit lives in you and me. If you have received him as your Saviour will you allow Him to reveal Himself through you, whatever the cost? We are now God's right hand to reach into a hurting world. He chose us for such a time as this, before the creation of the world. Don't settle for second best. God wants to give you the very best, but that will only come if you sow what you have. It's time to take God seriously.I firmly believe that revival is coming when Jesus will manifest Himself in powerful and awesome ways, and this will all come directly from His throne room as believers treat seriously their relationship with Jesus, putting Him and others before themselves. It will cost you your life and sadly, not all are willing to pay such a price, preferring to stay in a place of receiving, but giving very little, wanting to stay in control of their own lives. These visions are a picture of God's heart for His children. We have seen His glory in the form of Jesus Christ, to show us the way to know the King, so that on this rock the church can be built and the glory of God be revealed through you and me. His glory will come where Jesus is on the throne and where God is held in reverent fear.

11

Building the Temple

God is building His Temple, a place where He can live with His people, where His glory and goodness may be manifested and where this spiritual marriage can be established. The Bible says that we, as believers, *are* God's Temple and His Spirit lives in us (see 1 Cor.3:16). As we come to Him, the living stone, the Rock,

> '*we also, like living stones, are being built into a spiritual house to be a holy priesthood, offering spiritual sacrifices acceptable to God through Jesus Christ.*' 1 Peter 2:5.

This has been His plan from before the beginning of time and we are very close to its completion in these last days. As we are willing, God will slot us in together to form one body, so that the world will be impacted by the glory of God. He wants to build strong temples that will last and be effective in His purposes. In my home church – Kingdom Faith Church in Horsham – our pastor, Colin Urquhart, gave us some excellent teaching on building the Temple. I became very excited when I heard and saw how it related to the visions that the Lord had given to me. Imagine a temple, where the foundations are made of a number of stones, on which are built four pillars to support the roof and the walls, which hold the doors and windows. This temple, which is you, *must* have firm foundations in Christ.

> *'For no-one can lay any foundation other than the one already laid, which is Jesus Christ.'* 1 Cor. 3:11.

Jesus is the Word of God, and the foundations consist of revelation of three things found in God's Word, the Bible.The first layer: Revelation of the cross and what God has *already* accomplished in Christ. The work of the cross is foundational to everything God builds. The second layer: Revelation of our position in Christ, of who we are in Him. We are accepted, loved and seated with Him in heavenly places.The third layer: Revelation of what we have inherited because of what Jesus did on the cross. We are co-heirs with Jesus, the old has gone, the new has come, and we have eternal life.Once the foundations are in place and strong, we can then start to build, beginning with the four supporting pillars.

The first pillar that needs to be established in our spiritual lives is holiness, being set apart for God's purposes.

> *'Without holiness no-one will see the Lord.'* Heb *12:14. 'As obedient children, do not conform to the evil desires you had when you lived in ignorance. But just as he who called you is holy, so be holy in all you do; for it is written: "Be holy, because I am holy."'* 1 Peter 1:14–16.

God requires holiness, but do we really want it? We can only put aside the things of the world and be holy if we truly desire this.The second pillar to be built is the pillar of faith, for we cannot live a holy life without faith.

'... without faith it is impossible to please God.' (Heb.11:6).

Faith is based on God's Word and what He has done, not on what is happening around us or man's opinion.

'Faith comes from hearing the message, and the message is heard through the word of Christ.' Rom. 10:17.

Faith is choosing to believe what the Bible says. The third pillar is the pillar of love, because faith has to be worked out through love.

'If I speak in the tongues of men and angels, but have not love, I am only a resounding gong or a clanging cymbal. If I have the gift of prophecy and can fathom all mysteries and all knowledge, and if I have a faith that can move mountains, but have not love, I am nothing. If I give all I possess to the poor and surrender my body to the flames, but have not love, I gain nothing.' 1Cor. 13:1–3.

"A new command I give you: Love one another. As I have loved you, so you must love one another. By this all men will know that you are my disciples, if you love one another." John 13:34–35.

When we are secure in the love of Jesus because of what He has done and who He is, and not dependant upon our feelings or circumstances, we are able to love others. And the fourth pillar is the pillar of power – the power of the Holy Spirit.

"But you will receive power when the Holy Spirit comes on you; and you will be my witnesses in Jerusalem, and in all Judea and Samaria, and to the ends of the earth." Acts1:8.

We cannot do any of the things that God asks of us by ourselves. Praise God that His Word says, *'My grace is sufficient for you, for my power is made perfect in weakness.'* 2 Cor.12:9.

We need to surrender to Him, acknowledging that we need Him and can do nothing without Him.Do you ever wonder where that power of God is in *your* life? You are born again and baptised in the Holy Spirit, so that means you have also received His power. Where is it? You may well ask. All the ingredients or necessary materials are there, but they need to be utilised in the construction of the temple. All four pillars are vital to our spiritual growth and must be built up together and of equal height, otherwise the roof will be unequally supported. Begin with the pillar of holiness, because pollution in the temple will stop the flow of power, love and faith. The more we surrender and co-operate with the Holy Spirit, the faster and further we can grow. How large do you want your temple to be? How much of God's glory do you want in your life? The answer will be determined by how much you co-operate with Him in the building process. The higher the pillars are raised, the more space will be available to be filled with glory and power. But remember that *you* cannot do it, only God can, and He will do it only if you co-operate.The Lord says to you, "Just love Me, _____," (insert your own name here), "just love me, and everything else will flow from that." When the Lord said that to me, it felt as if a great weight had been lifted from my shoulders. I had been hearing such wonderful teaching about having faith, believing and obeying and yet I seemed to be failing miserably. "How come others can do it and I can't?" Then I realised that 'I' don't have to because 'I' cannot. All I have to do is love Him, and even that is only made possible for me by the power of the Holy Spirit. The walls of the temple represent godly wisdom to keep out the darkness and influences of this world and to keep in what the Lord puts in, such as love and peace. Some of the windows represent your eyes, which let the light shine in or out. *"If your eyes are good, your whole body will be full of light."* Matt. 6:22.

Be careful what you look at. Fix your eyes upon Jesus and not on worldly or evil things, being especially careful what you watch on television. The rest of the windows represent your ears, so take care what you listen to. Listen to the truth of God's Word rather than to gossip, criticism, condemnation or lies of the enemy. If you are constantly seeing or hearing arguments, violence or negativity, then that is what will influence you. *"Out of the overflow of the heart the mouth speaks."* Matt. 12:34. What has gone into your heart and mind will flow out of your mouth, which is represented by the temple door. Use your lips to praise and declare the glory of God. Set a guard on your mouth. Out of the temple doors flows the river of life, the living waters of holiness, faith, love and power. Are the pillars in place? Are you compromising in any way? What is going out from you and what is coming in? Are light and life flowing from you?

This teaching on building the pillars reminds me of the last of my four visions in which I climbed the mountain. To climb, we need two hands and two feet. In other words, the whole person has to climb to reach the presence of God and the fullness of His plan for you. You cannot climb with only one hand and one foot, or with one hand and two feet, or even with two hands and one foot. If you don't use both your hands and both your feet, you will not go any higher, or you may possibly fall.

The first hand, as you take hold of the rock to reach up to God, represents holiness. *'If the part of the dough offered as first fruits is holy, then the whole batch is holy; if the root is holy, so are the branches.'* Rom. 11:16. That first hand to reach out is the desire and the willingness to be set apart for God, to be right with Him, realising that we need to change. It requires repentance, a change of focus, to turn away from sin and worldly things and to turn back to God. All it takes initially is a desire to be right with God, followed by a step of faith. The hand reaches out, followed by the first foot, which represents the pillar of faith being built in your life. Without faith, you cannot live a holy life and you cannot please God. Faith gives you the push that you need to climb.

'I am not ashamed of the gospel, because it is the power of God for the salvation of everyone who believes: first for the Jew, then for the Gentile. For in the gospel a righteousness from God is revealed, a righteousness that is by faith from first to last, just as it is written: "The righteous will live by faith."' Rom. 1:16–17.

The righteous (those made right with and set apart for God through Jesus) will live by faith.

"I tell you the truth, anyone who has faith in me will do what I have been doing. He will do even greater things than these, because I am going to the Father." John 14:12.

The first hand, of holiness, is on the rock, followed by faith taking a foothold and next the hand of love reaches out to take a grip.

'Dear friends, let us love one another, for love comes from God. Everyone who loves has been born of God and knows God. Whoever does not love does not know God, because God is love. This is how God showed his love among us: He sent his one and only Son into the world that we might live through him. This is love: not that we loved God, but that he loved us and sent his Son as an atoning sacrifice for our sins. Dear friends, since God so loved us, we also ought to love one another. No-one has ever seen God; but if we love one another, God lives in us.' 1 John 4:7–12. *'We love because he first loved us. If anyone says, "I love God," yet hates his brother, he is a liar. For anyone who does not love his brother, whom he has seen, cannot love God, whom he has not seen. And he has given us this command: Whoever loves God must also love his brother.'* 1 John 4:19–21.

The love of God spurs us on and up, and because He first loved us, as we receive the revelation of that, we can love others. You are to be an expression of God's love in the world. As we draw near to God and love Him, His love will flow through us to others.Finally, the other foot kicks in with the power, *His* power. The Lord said to the Apostle Paul:

"My grace is sufficient for you, for my power is made perfect in weakness." 2 Cor.12:9.

Paul knew that he could do nothing by himself and it had to be the Lord's power and strength which enabled him to overcome the hard times – the difficult parts of the climb. He went on to say,

> *'Therefore I will boast all the more gladly about my weaknesses, so that Christ's power may rest on me. That is why, for Christ's sake, I delight in weaknesses, in insults, in hardships, in persecutions, in difficulties. For when I am weak, then I am strong."* 2 Cor.12:9–10. *'(He) is able to do immeasurably more than all we ask or imagine, according to his power that is at work within us.'* Eph. 3:20.

You cannot live a holy life, you cannot walk in faith and you cannot love others or know the King, unless the Holy Spirit, the power of God, enables you to do so.

> *'Faith by itself, if it is not accompanied by action, is dead.'* James 2:17.

That '*action*' means living life in obedience to God, loving others by serving them and allowing God's power to flow through us. And without love, nothing else means a thing, as faith works through love. If all your hands and feet don't work together, where will you be? The answer is that you will still be at the bottom of the mountain looking up; still in the outer court at a distance, not seeing the power of the resurrected life. First hand – first foot – second hand – second foot, then the first hand again, followed by the first foot, followed by the second hand and so on, climbing higher and higher up the mountain of God. The higher you climb, the more you will encounter and be engulfed in the presence and glory of God. With every act of obedience, each step of faith, every time you reach out with the hand of love, and whenever you surrender to the Holy Spirit's power flowing through you, your spiritual muscles are strengthened, enabling you to go on.

"Whoever has my commands and obeys them, he is the one who loves me. He who loves me will be loved by my Father, and I too will love him and show myself to him." John 14:21. And what is the greatest commandment? *"Love the Lord your God with all your heart and with all your soul and with all your mind and with all your strength."* Mark 12:30.

The whole person, body, soul and spirit, has to climb the mountain. Ask yourself: do I truly love God with my whole being?

In John, chapter twenty-one, Jesus asked Simon Peter three times if he loved Him. Twice He asked, "Simon, son of John, do you truly love me?" The Greek word for love used here was 'agape', which means to truly love with the whole person, a Godly love. Each time, Simon Peter answered, "You know that I love you," but he used the Greek word, 'philo', meaning a natural human affection which is based more on the emotions, a brotherly love. Jesus wanted Peter to know that there was a greater love that was not based on circumstances, moods or emotions; an intimate oneness; a *knowing*, as between a husband and wife, that He also wants for you and for me. God wants us to have a love relationship with Jesus that is far greater and deeper than anything we have previously experienced, and which many Christians sadly never attain. Peter did later find real 'agape' love, but only after he came to realise that without

93

Jesus, there is *nothing*. This place with Jesus is only ever found after the most difficult parts of the climb and the realisation that in our own strength we will fail.

> *'If any man builds on this foundation using gold, silver, costly stones, wood, hay or straw, his work will be shown for what it is, because the Day will bring it to light. It will be revealed with fire, and the fire will test the quality of each man's work. If what he has built survives, he will receive his reward. If it is burned up, he will suffer loss; he himself will be saved, but only as one escaping through the flames.'* 1 Cor.3:12–15.

There is no easy way or shortcut to the presence of God, or to becoming strong well-built temples which will contain His presence. If you try to take shortcuts, grabbing a quick snatch of time here, tossing up the odd prayer there, or just doing things for the sake of appearances, then it will be like building with wood, hay or straw. When the difficult times come, you will fall and suffer loss. You will still be saved but *only as one escaping through the flames* and you will not receive your reward. If you didn't have to actually do the climb yourself, you would not become strong or build up your spiritual muscles, and this is why you have to climb the mountain and build the temple, learning through circumstances, even through pain and suffering, making right choices and choosing to trust the Lord as you go. He is faithful!

12

From Beginning To End

Part One

The Beginning

I know that the teaching of our church pastor, Colin Urquhart, about building the Temple is God's heart, because the Lord revealed to me that it is exactly what He has been doing since time began. He has been building His Temple to contain His glory and to prepare the bride for Christ.

> '"Come, I will show you the bride, the wife of the Lamb." And he carried me away in the Spirit to a mountain great and high, and showed me the Holy City, Jerusalem, coming down out of heaven from God. It shone with the glory of God, and its brilliance was like that of a very precious jewel, like a jasper, clear as crystal.' Rev. 21:9–11.

The whole of the Bible is to teach us and show us what the Lord's will is. Everything is outlined in the Word of God, both in His personal plan for our lives and His bigger plan for the whole of creation.

> 'And he made known to us the mystery of his will according to his good pleasure, which he purposed in Christ, to be put into effect when the times will have

reached their fulfilment—to bring all things in heaven and on earth together under one head, even Christ. In him we were also chosen, having been predestined according to the plan of him who works out everything in conformity with the purpose of his will.' Eph. 1:9–11. *'In the beginning God created the heavens and the earth.'* Gen 1:1. *'And God said, "Let there be light," and there was light. God saw that the light was good ...'* v. 3–4.

He separated the light from the darkness, making day and night. He made the land and the seas, plants and trees, the sun, the moon and the stars. He filled the waters with living creatures and the sky with birds, and then He made the animals, the livestock and all creatures that move along the ground. All the living things He created '*according to their kind*', to be fruitful and to increase in number.

'And God saw that it was good.' 'Then God said, "Let us make man in our image, in our likeness, and let them rule ... " So God created man in his own image, in the image of God he created him; male and female he created them. God blessed them and said to them, "Be fruitful and increase in number; fill the earth and subdue it." ... God saw all that he had made, and it was very good. And there was evening, and there was morning—the sixth day.' Gen.1:26–31.

The very last thing that God created, at the end of the sixth day, was man, His masterpiece. The earth and everything else were created first, in readiness, and then God made man and put him on earth to rule, take care of it and have authority over the animals.

'Thus the heavens and the earth were completed in all their vast array. By the seventh day God had finished the work he had been doing; so on the seventh day he rested from all his work. And God blessed the seventh day and made it holy, because on it he rested from all the work of creating that he had done.' Gen. 2:1–3.

God rested on the seventh day, because everything was done; the work was finished. All He had to do now was wait: wait for everything to be fruitful and increase in the fullness of time, exactly as He planned. God had done all that He needed to do. Now creation itself had to take its course according to the predestined plan and purpose of God's will. God was not surprised when Adam sinned. He didn't think, "Oh no, everything has gone wrong, now I'll have to come up with another plan." There was never a plan 'B'. He knew it all before it happened. He knew when He created the angels that the most beautiful one, Lucifer, (or Satan), who led the worship, would become so full of pride that he would turn against Him. Many Bible interpreters believe that a third of the angels joined in the rebellion against God and were thrown from Heaven, together with Satan. God knew exactly how man would react when Satan tempted him. He didn't cause it to happen, but He certainly knew that it would.

'Now the LORD God had planted a garden in the east, in Eden; and there he put the man he had formed. And the LORD God made all kinds of trees grow out of the ground – trees that were pleasing to the eye and good for food. In the middle of the garden were the tree of life and the tree of the knowledge of good and evil.' Gen. 2:8–9.

'The LORD God took the man and put him in the Garden of Eden to work it and take care of it. And the LORD God commanded the man, "You are free to eat from any tree in the garden; but you must not eat from the tree of the knowledge of good and evil, for when you eat from it you will surely die." Gen. 2:15–17.

Why were there two trees in the Garden of Eden? If God knew that man would disobey Him, why did He plant the tree of the knowledge of good and evil and not just the tree of life? Wouldn't it have been easier? It *had* to happen this way; God wanted a family, a bride for Christ, who would *choose* to love Him. Adam and Eve walked with God in the garden, where they had everything they required and a wonderful relationship with God, but that's all they knew. They didn't know what they were choosing. I believe that God wanted something deeper and more intimate; He wanted a family who would love Him with all their heart, soul, mind and strength. God said that *when* they ate from the tree of the knowledge of good and evil, they *would surely* die. In other words – *when* they disobeyed God they *would* be separated from Him. Do you see? Man *had* to be separated from God, otherwise it would be impossible for him to *'grasp how wide and long and high and deep is the love of Christ and to know this love that surpasses knowledge – that* [they] *may be filled to the measure of all the fullness of God.'* Eph.3:18 and 19. God's plan is to fill us with the fullness of His goodness and His glory, by the power of His Holy Spirit.

'Then God said, "Let us make man in our image, in our likeness ... " So God created man in his own image, in the image of God he created him; male and

female he created them.' Gen.1:26–27. Then the Lord said, *"It is not good for the man to be alone. I will make a helper suitable for him."* Gen. 2:18. *'So the man gave names to all the livestock, the birds of the air and all the beasts of the field. But for Adam no suitable helper was found. So the LORD God caused the man to fall into a deep sleep; and while he was sleeping, he took one of the man's ribs and closed up the place with flesh. Then the LORD God made a woman from the rib he had taken out of the man, and he brought her to the man. The man said, "This is now bone of my bones and flesh of my flesh; she shall be called 'woman', for she was taken out of man." For this reason a man will leave his father and mother and be united to his wife, and they will become one flesh.'* Gen.2:20–24.

God wanted a family; He wanted a bride for Christ, someone to be totally 'one' with Him. He wanted children. This has always been in His heart. We were in His heart from the beginning. He had a plan, and so He painted a picture, to demonstrate and show us how that was going to happen. When Adam (man) was created, he was made in the image of God, complete, and woman was already *'in'* him. The Lord God then caused Adam to fall into a deep sleep while He removed a rib and formed the woman. Woman was taken out of man and then they were re-united to become one flesh, man and wife. Please note here that the woman was taken out of man, so God also called her Adam, meaning 'man' or 'mankind' – they were equal in His sight. It was Adam who named her woman.

'In the beginning was the Word, and the Word was with God, and the Word was God. He was with God in the

beginning. Through him all things were made; without him nothing was made that has been made. In him was life, and that life was the light of men.' John 1:1–4.

Jesus is the 'Word', He was there in the beginning, He knew us before the creation of the world; we were in Him, in His heart and plan. We were then separated or taken from Him through sin, becoming independent of God, and then through Jesus' death on the cross, we were re-united with God and made one with Him. We are the 'bride' of Christ. We are His betrothed and being prepared as a bride beautifully dressed for her husband.

'Praise be to the God and Father of our Lord Jesus Christ, who has blessed us in the heavenly realms with every spiritual blessing in Christ. For he chose us in him before the creation of the world to be holy (set apart for Him) *and blameless* (forgiven and made right with Him) *in his sight. In love he predestined us to be adopted as his sons* (God's children) *through Jesus Christ, in accordance with his pleasure and will – to the praise of his glorious grace, which he has freely given us in the One he loves.* (It is all a work of His grace, and not anything that we could ever earn.) *In him we have redemption through his blood, the forgiveness of sins, in accordance with the riches of God's grace that he lavished on us with all wisdom and understanding. And he made known to us the mystery of his will according to his good pleasure, which he purposed in Christ, to be put into effect when the times will have reached their fulfilment – to bring all things in heaven and on earth together under one head, even Christ.'* Eph.1:3–10

In Genesis chapter two, it is written that the heavens and the earth were completed in all their vast array, and yet the Bible only seems to describe the creation of the earth. Although this is a rather unusual interpretation of Scripture, I believe that the Garden of Eden was a 'heavenly place' and at the fall of man, that too was separated from the earth. The mystery of God's will, to be put into effect when the times have reached their fulfilment, is to bring all things in heaven and on earth together under one head, our husband, even Christ. The bride will have made herself ready.

'In him we were also chosen, having been predestined according to the plan of him who works out everything in conformity with the purpose of his will, in order that we, who were the first to hope in Christ, (who is our only hope) *might be for the praise of his glory. And you also were included in Christ when you heard the word of truth, the gospel of your salvation. Having believed, you were marked in him with a seal, the promised Holy Spirit, who is a deposit guaranteeing our inheritance until the redemption of those who are God's possession – to the praise of his glory.'* Eph. 1:11–14.

'Surely the Sovereign LORD does nothing without revealing his plan to his servants the prophets.' Amos 3:7.

It seems to be a pattern throughout the Bible that the Lord shows or reveals events in some way, before they take place. Look at the stories of Joseph and Moses. Your life is no different: God may show you something, people may prophesy over your life, or you may even get a foretaste of doing a specific task for a while, but then everything seems to go in totally the opposite direction. The dream God has given you or the word spoken over you seem to go so far out of reach that it all appears impossible, but be encouraged! If God has said it, it *will* come to pass, no matter how ridiculous, or how far out of reach, no matter what the circumstances, whether or not you think that you are able to do something, if God has said it, in *His* time and in *His* way, it will take place. If you think that you are ready and able, and cannot understand what is causing the delay, then the likelihood is that you are *not* ready. Only God knows when everything is in place, but it *will* happen.

> *'However, as it is written: "No eye has seen, no ear has heard, no mind has conceived what God has prepared for those who love him" – but God has revealed it to us by his Spirit … .We have not received the spirit of the world but the Spirit who is from God, that we may understand what God has freely given us.'*
> 1 Cor. 2:9–10 and 12.

This is all about our relationship with God through Jesus, in the power of His Holy Spirit, as the bride is prepared for the day when Jesus returns. He's already given us everything we need, but we can only walk in the good of it when we receive revelation from God and then act upon it. (Remember the gift box in an earlier chapter?)

In my early days as a student at Bible College, I dreamt that I was getting married. I had the wedding dress, but it wasn't quite right. It was passable, although not really what I would choose, but it would have to do. Two adult bridesmaids walked in. They both had dresses that didn't quite match, but I decided that they also would have to do.

Suddenly, the scene changed and I was with my mother at the hairdresser's, becoming very tense. "I have to get my hair done; I must get it done," I was saying, and the hairdresser replied very reluctantly, "Well, I suppose I'll have to do it." She was obviously not the slightest bit interested. "And I haven't got a veil or a head-dress yet," I panicked. "There are some over there, I suppose you'd better borrow one of those," came her bored reply, as she pointed to a couple of rather crumpled veils and head-dresses. The scene changed again. This time I found myself in a chilly old village hall with very rough, bare, splintery floorboards and peeling paint. The guests were beginning to arrive, and I was becoming more and more disappointed and worried. "Where's the hair-dresser?" I cried out in frustration. "Where is she? She promised she'd do my hair." At this point in the dream, I woke up shouting, "Grrrr, everything is all wrong, I can't get it right." Following this dream, the next day in our church service, we had a time of receiving from God. As I stood with my eyes closed and hands held out waiting, in a vision the Lord handed me a wedding dress – a beautiful wedding dress, the perfect dress. Then I saw a group of bridesmaids posing for a photograph, all with matching dresses, and the Lord said to me, "You don't have to make do with second best, because I am going to give you the best." It never entered my head at the time that the Lord was telling me He was going to give me a husband. I had gone to the college to get to know God, not to find a husband, so I saw it simply as God saying that He wants to give His children the best, which of course He does. God showed me what He was going to do, but it wasn't until much later that I realised, and in the meantime I was fighting it all the way, rebuking the devil for distracting me from what I had gone to the college to do. Before Gerry and I were eventually married, I had called off the relationship four times, running scared, but that's another story. God separated me for Himself until I was submitted and ready for whatever *His* will was, and then *He* brought it into being – *exactly* as He had first shown me. He gave me the wedding dress – I had the pick of any dress in the bridal shop, totally free – I had five bridesmaids, all with matching dresses, and a pageboy. I realised later that both my dress and the bridesmaids' dresses were the ones that I had seen in my vision. The person who was going to do my hair and provide the head-dress and veil was unable to come at the last minute, so I had an emergency appointment at the hairdresser, and the Lord provided a long veil and a tiara for me – my crown. And most wonderful of all, He gave me the best husband – God's choice for me.

Recently, during another time of receiving during worship, I had my hands held out and in a vision, I saw the Lord giving me my wedding dress again, – *exactly* the same as He did almost seven years to the day before. But this time He said,

"Rose, when I gave you that wedding dress, it wasn't just about you getting married to Gerry. It was also about being the bride of Christ, about being in intimacy and oneness with Me and having a passionate love relationship. And out of that passionate oneness you will give birth and you will reproduce and be fruitful. There *will* be a harvest."The next day He reminded me of this again and continued the conversation saying, "I have given you the wedding dress as my bride – the white robes, but *you* have to put them on and wear them and also put on the precious jewels." Later, to confirm the word, He also gave me various Scriptures:

"'Let us rejoice and be glad and give him glory! For the wedding of the Lamb has come, and the bride has

made herself ready. Fine linen, bright and clean, was given her to wear." (Fine linen stands for the righteous acts of the saints.)' Rev.19:7 and 8.

The garments were *given* to her to wear, just as the wedding dress was given to me. This text speaks of the promise of restored intimacy with God after the bride has made herself ready for Him by submitting and being cleansed by the washing of His Word, so that she can be presented to the Bridegroom without spot, wrinkle or blemish.

'I saw the Holy City, the new Jerusalem, coming down out of heaven from God, prepared as a bride beautifully dressed for her husband. And I heard a loud voice from the throne saying, "Now the dwelling of God is with men, and he will live with them."' Rev.21:2 and 3.

The 'Holy City', the 'new Jerusalem', refers to God's people, the Temple – His bride beautifully dressed for her husband, and once again, restored intimacy. We are talking about revival here, a revival that is surely coming, as God's temple is built.

'I delight greatly in the LORD; my soul rejoices in my God. For he has clothed me with garments of salvation and arrayed me in a robe of righteousness, as a bridegroom adorns his head like a priest, and as a bride adorns herself with her jewels. For as the soil makes the young plant come up and a garden cause seeds to grow, so the Sovereign LORD will make righteousness and praise spring up before all nations.' Isaiah.61:10 and 11.

To put on the wedding dress/white robes that God has given to us is to put on holiness and obedience, to surrender our lives and make a commitment to live in righteousness and the fear of the Lord and in covenant relationship with others, adorning ourselves with precious jewels, as it were. He *saved* us and *gave* us holy lives, set apart for Him. The temple building is to be constructed on the foundations of Christ and what He has done, using gold, silver and precious stones, materials which are durable and will not be burned up in the times of testing, and these materials symbolise sound doctrine and a holy submitted lifestyle. When we put on the wedding dress/white robes (our lifestyle), we are drawing closer and becoming more intimately involved with our Lord. *Then* the soil of our lives will be fertile and the produce will appear. Our lives will become fruitful and *then* we will live in freedom. *Then* we will see things happen. *Then* the love light of Jesus will radiate from us, drawing others into the Kingdom. *Then,* revival will come. All through the Bible, God has been showing us how to put on the wedding dress and how to build the temple that is to contain His glory. All through time He has used different people to demonstrate to us what was required and to draw us to Himself.

13

From Beginning To End

Part Two

The Challenge of Faith

As I have said previously, God wants a people who are set apart for Himself. To show what is necessary for this, we begin with a man of faith, Abraham, the man known as the 'Father of faith' because he showed faith in times of disappointment, trial and testing. Because of his faith, God counted him as righteous, that is, right in His eyes.

> *'Abraham believed God, and it was credited to him as righteousness.'* Rom. 4:3. *'Against all hope, Abraham in hope believed.'* Rom. 4:18

The Lord God made a covenant, an agreement, with Abraham. He promised to bless him, to make his name great, and to bless all peoples on earth through him, but there was a condition. If you do this ... you will open the way for Me to do this ... It was not intended as a condition for earning the blessings, but simply to open the way.

> *'The LORD had said to Abram, "Leave your country, your people and your father's household and go to the land I will show you. I will make you into a great nation and I will bless you; I will make your name*

great, and you will be a blessing. I will bless those
who bless you, and whoever curses you I will curse;
and all peoples on earth will be blessed through
you."' Gen. 12:1–3

Abraham was faced with a choice: would he leave his home, his friends and everything he knew to go to another place, or would he stay where he was? Would he stay in the security of what he knew and had, or would he let go and step out into the unknown, trusting God to direct him as He had promised? This was the same decision that I was faced with at YWAM before going to Uganda for the first time, as I told you in chapter 8. Was I going to step out in faith, choosing to trust God, or was I going to stay safe and do nothing? I told you how my decision to go not only changed my life but would also in time affect the lives of many others.

All I had known about YWAM before I went there was that they had a hospital ship called the Anastasis and a building in Nuneaton, Warwickshire. (For those who don't know, 'Youth with a Mission' is a huge worldwide organisation.) I had gone to their 'Crossroads Weekend' because my daughter had now left home and I felt I was at a crossroads in my life, ... then suddenly I was faced with this decision. Was I going to step out of the boat and really trust God, even though I was afraid, or was I going to play safe? It felt almost as though God had tricked me to get me to this place, or as my husband would say, "God stitched me up."Abraham couldn't possibly have comprehended how important his decision was, whether to go or stay, but his step of faith affected the history of the whole world. His decision started the development of God's people, and the ancestral line through which Jesus would come. Through

Abraham's decision the whole world would be blessed. When we make decisions like this, we don't know what the long-term effects will be, but the Lord does. He is the author and finisher of our faith. Like Abraham, I too never dreamed where my step of faith would lead, what would develop from it, or who would be affected by my decision to go. There were twelve of us in our group, and I was probably the least experienced of the lot and one of the most nervous, having had quite a culture shock. I was the last person anyone would have expected to go somewhere like that, let alone return there, but God changed my life on that trip and started the development of something that I could never have imagined. Because I had no experience of preaching or teaching, for most of the eight-week trip I was only allowed to give testimony, until the last Sunday that we were there. That day, three of us were sent to a fishing village on the edge of Lake Victoria to speak in a little grass thatched, mud built church. The three of us who went were probably the least of the group, sent to a place that few people had ever heard of, to a church and a pastor that no-one seemed too bothered about. It was just somewhere to send us, and to top that, even though I had not done any teaching or preaching before, I was the main speaker –wow! That little church was full of people, hungry to hear from God, and He was not about to disappoint them. From the moment they started to praise and worship, the presence of God was there, and by the time I got up to speak it felt as though I were wading through water as I walked towards the lectern. God's presence was so thick that I could have been a cardboard cut-out for all the difference I made, He did it all. It was the most amazing experience and one that I will never forget. The Bible says that sign and wonders will follow the preaching of God's Word, and they did. People were healed, saved and delivered, and best of all, they met with Almighty God. I felt as though I could have taken off and flown that day, indeed, I suppose I did in the Spirit! Anything was possible! I was speaking, or rather, the Lord was speaking through me, about entering into the presence of God in the Holy of Holies and spending time with Him there. That night, so I discovered later, the whole church stayed in the building all night to seek more of the presence of God. That had to be God! Because we knew that something very special had happened, the pastor, Dan Kayondo, and I kept in touch by letter, and after a time he began to tell me about the big brick built church that he believed the Lord had told him to build. I later discovered that he had actually sold everything he owned to lay the foundations and many people mocked and laughed at him for building such a big church in a place like Kiyindi, but just like Noah building the ark, Pastor Dan knew that he had heard from God. I really wanted to help him with the costs, but I had no money left.

After returning to England, the Lord directed me to Kingdom Faith Bible College where I met Gerry, and once I had finally accepted that God had put us together, a little daydream began to pop into my mind. 'Wouldn't it be nice if we could have an open, evangelistic outreach wedding in our own church where anyone and everyone was invited, raise some money there, then take the wedding dress to Uganda for another evangelistic outreach / wedding celebration, give them the money and say, "Here's your church." Well, what began as a daydream became reality. That is exactly what happened – with a lot of exciting miracles on the way. It was wonderful … but that's another story. The following year, Gerry and I visited Uganda again to see how the church was progressing. While we were there we met a young boy named Julius whose face was badly scarred from a fire in his hut a few years before. He looked a sorry sight as he stood before us dressed in dirty rags, with his head down not wanting to look at us, or more probably not wanting us to look at him. The scars pulled his mouth almost inside out down his neck, making movement difficult. As he was growing up, it was also affecting his breathing. Again, we wanted to help, but didn't know how, so all we did was take photographs of him, brought them back to England and God did the rest. It's a long story and again there were many miracles along the way, but basically he came and stayed with us for eleven months in England and had plastic surgery to release his neck. When we took him back he had grown six inches, walked with his head high and an African swagger. He was also saved, baptised in water and filled with the Holy Spirit. God is good! When we took Julius back to his home, the Lord told us to buy a plot of land. "We haven't got enough money for a plot of land, Lord. And anyway, why would we want a plot of land in Kiyindi?" asked Gerry. We were surprised to find when we checked that we could scrape together £800, but that was everything we had between us. The Lord said to use what we had and then He came up with a really good plot for … the exact amount we had, surprise, surprise. We were to build a job skills training centre and a residential Bible College. Again, there is a long, long story, which I will not go into here, but the buildings are now almost complete. We also have two adjoining plots and believe to buy one more as the Lord provides, for a large Medical Centre with pharmacy. What I am trying to show you here is that just a simple decision to step out in faith as the Lord leads can affect whole communities. The face of Kiyindi is changing and many lives will be affected by the grace of God.

Sometimes when I look at what He is doing there, I am just in awe at His goodness. Like Abraham, I too couldn't possibly have imagined how important my decision was, whether to go or stay. I'm just so grateful that He made all this possible all the glory goes to Him, and there's much more still to come.Abraham's story is about a man called by God to co-operate in His plan for the salvation of mankind. The promise to bless both Abraham and all peoples on earth was God's plan, and Abraham's faith was shown by his co-operation as he learned to respond to God's word by faith, as we have to do if we are to know our King Abraham responded in faith to the first instruction from God, and knew God's presence as a result, so when the Lord told him that he would have a son from his own body, even though he was too old and that his descendants would be as numerous as the stars; because his faith had been encouraged, he believed. *'"... a son coming from your own body will be your heir." He took him outside and said, "Look up at the heavens and count the stars – if indeed you can count them." Then he said to him, "So shall your offspring be." Abraham believed the LORD, and he credited it to him as righteousness.'* Gen 15:4–6.Abraham believed for *twenty-five* long years before Isaac was born, when humanly speaking, it was totally impossible.

'Against all hope, Abraham in hope believed and so became the father of many nations, just as it had been said to him, "So shall your offspring be." Without weakening in his faith, he faced the fact that his body was as good as dead – since he was about a hundred years old – and that Sarah's womb was also dead. Yet he did not waver through unbelief regarding the promise of God, but was strengthened in his faith and

gave glory to God, being fully persuaded that God had power to do what he had promised.' Rom. 4:18–20.

"Hang on a minute," you may be saying. "It says there that Abraham didn't waver through unbelief. What about Ishmael? Wasn't he the result of doubt?" … No. God told Abraham that a son from his own body would be his heir, but there was no mention of Sarah in the first instance. Abraham didn't doubt the promise, but he tried to work it out for himself and help God … as we all do, but of course, God doesn't need our help, only our co-operation. In our own strength we can do nothing, but with God *nothing* is impossible. The Lord doesn't ask you to do anything that is hard, only impossible, so that there will be no doubt that it was He who did it. He *will* prepare you and equip you for what He wants, taking you onwards, one step at a time, to teach you and to build up your faith.

As a young Christian, I had a lovely friend called Bettine, who was a wonderful artist. After a while of seeing her work, I started to get this strange feeling that I too could paint, which seemed ridiculous at the time. I'd done a bit of painting way back when I was at school, using powder paints and I was in a fairly artistic job, but that didn't necessarily mean that I could paint. So apart from Bettine, who encouraged me to have a go, I didn't tell anyone. That year, for my birthday, even though he knew nothing of my plans, one of my brothers gave me an artist's easel. Then nine days later for Christmas, he gave me the most wonderful leather inlaid mahogany paint box, filled with everything I would need to paint in oils. He had been working for an art supplier, as foreman in the department that made the paint boxes and easels. That year, he was made redundant, so he made the easel and box and filled it with his samples. After Christmas, I found a picture that I liked, copied it and to my amazement discovered that I

113

could paint to quite a high standard. The Lord said to me, "If I tell you that you can do something, then you *can* do it, and I will supply everything you need to do it." This was a lesson I needed to learn, because although painting was something that I could easily experiment with in private, God was about to challenge me to step out in faith in front of everyone in the church.I used to joke that where my singing voice was concerned, it went up when it should go down, down when it should go up and slid around in the middle. One day as I was driving along, singing to the Lord at the top of my voice, out of earshot of everyone else, I laughed and said, "Oh, Lord, I wish You'd do something with my voice, at least so that I can sing to You." The incident was then promptly forgotten. Shortly after this, during an evening service, we had a time of open prayer aimed at praising God. It was one of those times when everyone is sitting down quietly with their eyes closed, not like the noisy prayer meetings I'm used to now. Someone prayed, then silence, then another prayer – and silence. All the time I was fighting a strong desire to sing, and as what seemed like hours passed, the desire became stronger and stronger. With my heart thumping so loudly that the whole church *must* have heard and my mouth opening and closing like a goldfish, I knew that if I didn't do it I would explode. So with a deep breath and my eyes tightly closed as if to pretend that no-one else was there, the words of a well-known chorus came from my mouth:

> *'I love You, Lord, and I lift my voice,*
> *To worship You, O my soul, rejoice.*
> *Take joy, my King, in what You hear,*
> *Let me be a sweet, sweet sound in Your ear.'*

Laurie Klein, Copyright 1980
Thankyou Music, Eastbourne

Then, much to the amusement of everyone, came a surprised, "Lord, I can't believe I've just done that!" The amazing thing was that, although they all knew the song, *no-one* joined in, and what is more, it *was* a sweet sound … even to my ears. I couldn't believe it; not a note was out of place. The 'worship group' in this little Baptist church consisted of just four people: Beverley, who led the singing, Chris on bass guitar, another Chris on rhythm guitar and Shelley on flute, or singing or guitar if one of the others wasn't there. On the Friday evening, I went along to listen to the group practice, as I sometimes did to pass the time, but this time as I walked in, the four of them gave a cheer. It seemed that on the following Sunday morning, neither of the two girls would be there, so they had no singer. When they prayed about it, they believed that the Lord had said I was to do it and they decided that if I came that night then they would take it as confirmation. Well, the Lord went one better, as He does … I walked in at the very moment when they had just finished practising all the songs for the evening service, and were about to have to consider what would happen for the morning service. I was shocked but amazingly calm, and simply prayed, "Look, Lord, I'm willing, but You will have to do it because I can't. You are the potter and I am the clay, mould me and make me, this *is* what I pray." I didn't really understand what I was praying, it just seemed the right thing to say at the time. Beware; when you ask the Lord to mould you and make you, don't be surprised when things start to become uncomfortable, because He *will* hear you and answer your prayer. On the following Sunday, in spite of never having used a microphone before and *never* having sung in public, there I was, leading the worship. One week later, Beverley left the church and I was asked to join the group.God takes us one step at a time to build up our faith muscles. He tells us to do one thing, then when we obey that He gives us a bigger thing, then a bigger step, until our faith in Him is strong and we are able to be obedient to whatever He asks, knowing that He is faithful. ... Then He tests us to show *us* whether we really do believe and which is more important to us – the Giver or the gift.

> *'Then God said, "Take your son, your only son, Isaac, whom you love, and go to the region of Moriah. Sacrifice him there as a burnt offering on one of the mountains I will tell you about."'* Gen. 22:2.

What? Abraham had waited twenty-five years for the fulfilment of this promised son and heir. He was an old man now, so there wasn't likely to be another son and yet now he was being told to give him back. Isaac was the one through whom the promised blessings would come. It didn't make sense. This was the ultimate test of Abraham's faith and loyalty. Would he surrender his most prized possession? Who was more important to Abraham, God or Isaac? We know the story – at the crucial moment, the angel of the Lord stopped him and said,

> *"Now I know that you fear God, because you have not withheld from me your son, your only son."* Gen. 22:12.

I too was tested in a similar way, but we will talk about that later. This covenant with Abraham was a covenant of faith, which is one of the pillars of the temple that *must* be built in the lives of believers, if they are to *know* their King. God has a much better plan and a much closer walk with Jesus for us to undertake than any we could imagine, so it makes sense to surrender to Him, and trust that He really does know best. If we try to do it on our own, we will only succeed in obstructing God's best for us.

'Abraham believed God, and it was credited to him as righteousness.' Rom. 4:3.

Abraham's faith was credited to him as righteousness because it was true faith – complete confidence in God and His promises.

'Without faith it is impossible to please God, because anyone who comes to him must believe he exists and that he rewards those who earnestly seek him.' Heb. 11:6.

Faith is either a gift from God or fruit of the Spirit, either way it comes from Him. It is the faith *of* God and only comes when you realise your own helplessness and total dependence on Him.

14

From Beginning To End

Part Three

The Challenge of Holiness

Without faith, we cannot *please* God (see Heb. 11:6) and without holiness we cannot *see* God (see Heb 12:14). So the next thing that was necessary for mankind to understand, if they were to know this King, was the importance of holiness. Moses had a holy encounter with the great 'I AM' at the burning bush on the mountain. Because this experience had totally changed his life, his first port of call when he brought the children of Israel out of Egypt was the mountain, so that they too could have a life-changing encounter with God.

> *'In the third month after the Israelites left Egypt ... they entered the Desert of Sinai, and Israel camped there in the desert in front of the mountain. Then Moses went up to God, and the LORD called to him from the mountain and said, "This is what you are to say to the house of Jacob and what you are to tell the people of Israel: 'You yourselves have seen what I did to Egypt, and how I carried you on eagles' wings and brought you to myself. Now if you obey me fully and keep my covenant, then out of all nations you will be my treasured possession. Although the whole earth is*

mine, you will be for me a kingdom of priests and a holy nation."' Ex. 19:1–6.

The whole purpose of their coming out of captivity was to bring them to God, that they might become His treasured possession, a kingdom of priests and a holy nation, for the role of priests is to minister to God.

'And the LORD said to Moses, "Go to the people and consecrate them today and tomorrow. Make them wash their clothes and be ready by the third day, because on that day the LORD will come down on Mount Sinai in the sight of all the people."' Ex. 19:10–11.

Moses had brought the people out of Egypt, but the influence of Egypt was still in them. When you were saved, you came out of the world into a new place, and now you need to get the world out of you and be cleaned up, so that the world will see that you belong to Jesus. On the third day, He rose again from the dead to open the way and make that possible. The Bible says that each day is like a thousand years to the Lord. It is now two thousand years since Jesus lived on earth, which means that we are entering into the third day. The Lord Jesus is coming soon, and we need to be ready for Him.

'On the morning of the third day there was thunder and lightning, with a thick cloud over the mountain, and a very loud trumpet blast. Everyone in the camp trembled. Then Moses led the people out of the camp to meet with God, and they stood at the foot of the mountain. Mount Sinai was covered with smoke, because the Lord descended on it in fire. The smoke

billowed up from it like smoke from a furnace, the whole mountain trembled violently, and the sound of the trumpet grew louder and louder.' Ex. 19:16–19.

'When the people saw the thunder and lightning and heard the trumpet and saw the mountain in smoke, they trembled with fear. They stayed at a distance and said to Moses, "Speak to us yourself and we will listen. But do not have God speak to us or we will die." Moses said to the people, "Do not be afraid. God has come to test you, so that the fear of God will be with you to keep you from sinning." The people remained at a distance, while Moses approached the thick darkness where God was.' Ex. 20:18–21.

When God appeared on the mountain, the people could not stand it. Why? Because there was sin in their lives and because they had something to hide, so like Adam and Eve, they ran away in fear.

"For there is nothing hidden that will not be disclosed, and nothing concealed that will not be known or brought out into the open." Luke 8:17. *'But everything exposed by the light becomes visible.'* Eph.5:13.

Moses, like Abraham, was willing to approach the thick darkness where God was. *He* was willing to step into the unknown, but the people remained at a distance. These people had seen many miracles, as many people in our churches today see miracles. Even in this kind of atmosphere, sin can be hidden, but when the presence of God comes, sin is exposed.

"Many will say to me on that day, 'Lord, Lord, did we not prophesy in your name, and in your name drive out demons and perform many miracles?' Then I will tell them plainly, 'I never knew you. Away from me, you evildoers!'" Matt.7:22–23.

Aaron too was invited to climb the mountain, but he never went, because he feared the people more than he feared God.Here on Mount Sinai, God introduced another covenant for His people, one of obedience and holiness that was to cover every aspect of their lives, a complete picture of their lives as God's holy nation. At the centre of this covenant were the Ten Commandments, the Law.

"Now if you obey me fully and keep my covenant, then ... you will be my treasured possession." Ex.19:5.

In the coming move of God, His presence will be so strong that everything hidden will be exposed. Holiness is another pillar that *must* be built in our lives if we are to know our King intimately. It means to be completely dedicated to God and committed to His way of living rather than the world's way. It is being free from sin and wrongdoing, but more than that it is the presence of godliness and humility. When we become Christians, we are made holy by what Jesus did on the cross. He became sin for us, we were forgiven and made clean, and now God looks at us through Jesus, seeing us as if we had never sinned.

' ... Christ loved the church and gave himself up for her to make her holy, cleansing her by the washing with water through the word, and [presenting] her to himself as a radiant church, without stain or wrinkle

or any other blemish, but holy and blameless.' Eph. 5:25–27.

Having said this, even though God sees us as holy, holiness still needs to be perfected in our lives. Only when we get to heaven will we be completely holy, but we must still strive each day to be more like Jesus, our example, being changed from glory into glory.

'Since we have these promises, dear friends, let us purify ourselves from everything that contaminates body and spirit, perfecting holiness out of reverence for God.' 2 Cor. 7:1.

We grow in holiness by working hard to keep sin out of our lives as we learn the truths of the Bible and live by them. As the people of the Bible constantly realised, on our own we cannot do this because we were born into sin, but as we surrender ourselves more and more to God as living sacrifices, He will make us holy. It is a work of His Grace.

There was no doubt that it was the Lord who raised me up to lead worship in that first church, and it seemed to be the best thing that had ever happened to me. I grew to love the people and was very happy. Singing became my life. On Thursday evenings we practised with a Christian rock band, Friday night was worship practice, Saturday night would often be spent doing an outreach somewhere, and then on Sundays we practised before both services. My life was full of singing. The trouble was that not only did I become proud, but also the very gift that God had given me had become an idol. I was focusing more on the gift than the One for whom it was intended – Jesus. In fact, I was worshipping the worship rather than God.As time went on,

I moved to another church where, although I was still part of the worship team, it wasn't so important whether I was there or not, since they already had very good worship leaders. I went on to YWAM where I was faced with a similar situation, and I realised that I wasn't really so good after all. The old rejection was rearing its ugly head again, and yet I *knew* what God had done at the beginning. I really couldn't understand what was happening.When I came to Kingdom Faith, a church that is known for its worship, I joined the choir, and just to help things along as it were, I gave them my 'singing testimony'. Surely *then* they would see … I think I expected someone to say, "Wow, this is an amazing story! We should take notice, as God's hand is obviously upon this woman." … Of course, this didn't happen, because all I was doing, even though I didn't realise it at the time, was trying to promote myself and get myself accepted. I was also trying to *help* God to fulfil what I thought He had promised, as Abraham did with Hagar. Only God raises people up and you will only find true acceptance in *Him*, not in anything or anyone else. All I succeeded in doing was to cause myself more pain, rejection and embar-rassment, and to *close* the door – which obviously wasn't His door anyway. Every so often, an opportunity would arise for me to lead worship at a meeting somewhere. Then, just as suddenly, the door would slam in my face and I would be left asking, "Lord, I didn't seek this, You gave it to me, so why have You taken it away?" I was in turmoil. All the time this was going on, the Lord was using me in powerful ways, in many different places, *speaking* His word, healing the sick and encouraging others. This was great, but I couldn't seem to get past this one big obstacle and it was colouring everything. Which was more important to me – God or worship? … I didn't realise it at the time, but sadly for a while the answer to that question was worship. I had made an idol of the very thing that God had given to me and it took years of pain before I reached the point where I was willing to let it go. I praise God for His love that wouldn't let me stay in that wrong attitude. Eventually He brought me to a place where, with tears in my eyes, I was able to give away my microphone … and a dream. He said, "Rose, give me the 'dis-appointment' so that I can give you a 're-appointment'". The Lord had been put back in His rightful place, on the throne of my life. I learned the hard way … but thankfully, I learned. Only He knows what is best for our lives, and only He knows when we are truly ready with a right heart for His plans. Yes, God anointed me for that time, but it was only a small step in the plan He has for me, and I am only a small part in a much bigger plan. Sometimes we have to let go to move on to the better and more perfect plan that He has for us.

"You shall have no other gods before me." Ex. 20:3.

He will not tolerate any compromise. For my own sake, for the sake of others and for the sake of God's Name, I *had* to be broken. Incidentally, being broken before God is not a one-off event, it is something that has to take place regularly.If you truly want to know your King and move in to the fullness of His plan for you, ask Him to show you the areas in your life that are not pleasing to Him, repent (which means to turn around) and make a fresh commitment to go *His* way. If you don't do this, He may still use you to a degree, but it will be nothing compared to what He *wants* to move you into. There is so much more for you, and a deeper intimacy than you've ever known before Isaiah, chapter thirty-six, pictures God's final Kingdom and speaks of a highway, which will be called the Way of Holiness. The 'Life Application' Living Bible speaks of this 'Holy Highway' as being the way from the desert of suffering to the blessings of new life. It is found only by following Jesus.

'And a highway will be there; it will be called the Way of Holiness. The unclean will not journey on it; it will be for those who walk in that Way; wicked fools will not go about on it.' Isa. 35:8.

The Lord has prepared a way for us to walk *with* Him to His home. He doesn't just point the way, but walks *with* us *all* the way. Early one morning, immediately after I had awoken, as I lay in my bed, I asked the Lord, "How *do* I walk in holiness?" His answer came quickly, "Well Rose, to begin with, it means getting up and spending time with Me." To walk in holiness involves the discipline of spending time with the Lord. You cannot walk or live a holy life unless you first 'sit' with Him.

"Enter through the narrow gate. For wide is the gate and broad is the road that leads to destruction, and many enter through it. But small is the gate and narrow the road that leads to life, and only a few find it." Matt. 7:13–14.

Jesus is the way that was opened up for us. He is the *only* way to the Father, but not only is the gate narrow, so also is the road. Many people try to find their own way, thinking that they know what is best, but the Bible says to them,

'Trust in the LORD with all your heart and lean not on your own understanding; in all your ways

acknowledge him, and he will make your paths straight.' Prov. 3:5–6.

He will show you the right way – His way, which is not our way. To be obedient to God's way means to 'die' to your own. There was a time in my life when, after reading and hearing about 'dying to self', I found myself constantly thinking, "I must die to self. I really want to die to self. I *must* die to self." The trouble was that the more I said it, the more 'I' seemed to get in the way, until one day the Lord said to me, "Rose, forget about dying to self and concentrate on living for Jesus." It was like another burden being taken from my shoulders. The more I was telling myself that I must die, the more I was concentrating on myself and it is so much easier to live for Him than to kill yourself off. Jesus *calls* us to be holy and blameless in His sight. He made the way, and now all that is required is for us to believe it and live it. God is a God of detail and every detail of your life is important and needs to be given over to Him, so that He can bless you and you can *see* Him. Holiness apart from Him is impossible because He *is* Holiness.

'See to it, brothers, that none of you has a sinful, unbelieving heart that turns away from the living God. But encourage one another daily, as long as it is called Today, (while there is still time) *so that none of you may be hardened by sin's deceitfulness. We have come to share in Christ if we hold firmly till the end the confidence we had at first. As has been said: "Today, if you hear his voice, do not harden your hearts as you did in the rebellion." Who were they who heard and rebelled? Were they not all those Moses led out of Egypt? And with whom was he angry for forty*

years? Was it not with those who sinned, whose bodies fell in the desert? And to whom did God swear that they would never enter his rest if not to those who disobeyed? So we see that they were not able to enter, because of their unbelief. Therefore, since the promise of entering his rest still stands, let us be careful that none of you be found to have fallen short of it. For we also have had the gospel preached to us, just as they did; but the message they heard was of no value to them, because those who heard it did not combine it with faith ... Let us, therefore, make every effort to enter that rest, so that no-one will fall by following their example of disobedience. For the word of God is living and active. Sharper than any double-edged sword, it penetrates even to dividing soul and spirit, joints and marrow; it judges the thoughts and attitudes of the heart. Nothing in all creation is hidden from God's sight. Everything is uncovered and laid bare before the eyes of him to whom we must give account.' Heb. 3:12–4:13

15

From Beginning To End

Part Four

With Love – by Grace

> *'If I speak in the tongues of men and of angels, but have not love, I am only a resounding gong or a clanging cymbal. If I have the gift of prophecy and can fathom all mysteries and all knowledge, and if I have faith that can move mountains, but have not love, I am nothing. If I give all I possess to the poor and surrender my body to the flames, but have not love, I gain nothing.'* 1 Cor.13:1–3.

The covenant with Abraham showed God's plan for salvation and the need for faith to see that plan fulfilled. His covenant with Moses showed the quality of life that God expects from His saved people and the need for their lives to be holy and set apart for Him. Then this third covenant that He made with David was the promise of an everlasting Kingdom, it was a covenant of love. Out of David's line would be born a Saviour and through Him would come a Kingdom that would last forever, – a *marriage* that would last forever.

'For God so loved the world that he gave his one and only Son, that whoever believes in him shall not perish but have eternal life.' John 3:16.

This covenant was like a marriage proposal, and marriage requires the sharing of hearts and intimacy; without love, it will not last and means nothing. Because King Saul had not kept the command that the Lord gave him, God sought out a man with a heart after His own heart. (See 1 Sam. 13:14).

'The LORD does not look at the things man looks at. Man looks at the outward appearance, but the LORD looks at the heart.' 1 Sam. 16:7.

Anyone can *look* the part; it's what is in the heart that is important. David knew and loved God. As we can see in many of the psalms that he wrote, he had a heart for worship and a longing for God's presence. He wanted to bless God by building a house for Him, a magnificent temple. But the Lord said, "No, you are not the one to build a house for Me, *I* will establish a house, in *my* time and in *my* way, but I will establish it *through* you, because you have a heart after my own, and My house will last forever." (2 Sam.7:5–16 paraphrased). The Kingdom *must* be built in God's way and in God's time, not ours. This was an unconditional promise of the spiritual marriage that would surely happen, and yet at the same time the benefits of it were, and still are, conditional on faith, obedience and submission to God. It is love that enables us to believe, God's love in us, which, of course, springs from Him.

'Give ear and come to me; hear me, that your soul may live. I will make an everlasting covenant with

you, my faithful love promised to David.' Isa. 55:3.

Jesus said, *'If you love me, you will obey what I command.'* John 14:15.

A teacher of the Law asked Jesus, *"Of all the commandments, which is the most important?"* *"The most important one,"* answered Jesus, *"is this: 'Hear, O Israel, the Lord our God, the Lord is one. Love the Lord your God with all your heart and with all your soul and with all your mind and with all your strength.'* (in that order). *The second is this: Love your neighbour as yourself.' There is no commandment greater than these."* Mark 12:28–31.

"A new command I give you: Love one another. As I have loved you, so you must love one another. By this all men will know that you are my disciples, if you love one another." John 13:34–35.

God's whole plan from the beginning is that we should come into this love relationship with Him, and that none should be lost. His whole purpose for saving *you* is to draw others into his arms, so that we should be 'one' together. He knows that apart from Him we can do nothing. We cannot even love Him and neither can we love others as He commands. This is why Jesus teaches us in John's Gospel to remain in the vine.

"This is to my Father's glory, that you bear much fruit, showing yourselves to be my disciples. As the Father has loved me, so have I loved you. Now remain in my love. If you obey my commands, you will remain

in my love ... I have told you this so that my joy may be in you and that your joy may be complete. My command is this: Love each other as I have loved you. Greater love has no-one than this, that he lay down his life for his friends." John 15:8–13.

"Lord, give me a revelation of the Father's love. I need this revelation, I can't love others, I don't know how. I'm not even sure that I know what love is. Give me a revelation of the Father's love." ... For a long time I prayed this prayer, until one day, it was as though the penny dropped. Incidentally, have you noticed that we always expect revelation to be like a firework explosion? In fact, very often, it's more like the penny dropping and the answer just suddenly comes. ... The revelation of the Father's love comes through what comes out of us. We ask God, "Give me more love for the lost, so that I can obey this command and *do* more," because we know we can't do it without Him. Then we wonder why nothing changes, and He doesn't seem to have answered our prayer. We say, "You show me, Lord, and then I'll do it." And He says, "I've already shown you. I sent my Son and you already have all My love in you, so you act on it and then you will see the manifestation of My love for you coming out." *You* are part of the church, and the church is Christ's body here on earth. When *you* believe this and act on it, then yo*u* will see His love flowing through *you* to the nations. Jesus will be born through your line as He was through David's line.Love in itself is not a commodity; Jesus *is* the love of God and God wants to express Him through us. The love about which we are talking is not a feeling, although feelings will come, it's a decision we make. He will work it in us as we work it out.

"Just love Me, Rose," Jesus said to me, "Love Me and

132

everything else will come from that." *"If you love me you will obey what I command."* Jesus is not threatening us with a big stick in His hand, saying: "You *will* do as you are told." No, He is lovingly saying, "Don't you see, if you fall in love with Me, love Me with a passion as I love you, and I really do love you passionately, even to the point of dying for you, *then* out of that love relationship you will do the things I'm asking. That way it won't be hard at all, because you will want to do it. Everything in you will *want* to please Me." It all stems from that relationship, as we come to a place where we love *Him* more than we love ourselves, where we want *His* will before our own, confident that He really does know what's best for us. When someone falls in love, it shows. When you really love someone, you want to be with them as often as possible. You talk about them all the time and you want to do things for them … *"Simon, son of John, do you truly love me? … Feed My lambs … … Take care of my sheep."* Jacky Pullinger said, "Before you see the need, you *must see* the Lord, otherwise the need will screw you up." Isaiah *saw* the Lord. (See Isaiah, chap.6). He had an encounter with Jesus the King in His holiness, and this was followed by a revelation of a God who is loving and forgiving to cleanse him of his sin; and Isaiah was never the same again. When you receive a revelation of the Lord, you will also receive a revelation of who you are. You realise that He is almighty and awesome, and that in you there really is nothing good at all … *Then* He can *really* use you. I *did* see Jesus that day in a very powerful way. I saw Him in Jacky Pullinger … And I saw something in her that I wanted – a heart surrendered and submitted to Jesus, a heart after God's heart … and because of that, the Lord is using her in powerful ways. David made many mistakes and he was certainly not perfect. He messed up so many times, but quickly confessed his sins and repented. His confessions were from the heart and he knew God's forgiveness even though he had to suffer the consequences. He sought the Lord and spent time with the one he loved.

'One thing I ask of the LORD, this is what I seek: that I may dwell in the house of the LORD all the days of my life, to gaze upon the beauty of the LORD and to seek him in his temple.' Ps. 27:4.

(My favourite Bible verse)."Get up, Rose and come and spend some time with Me," the Lord said as He woke me in the early hours one morning. "Oh, Lord, do I have to? I'm really tired." I groaned. "Come on, a new day is dawning, watch with Me and see the sunrise," came the reply. I knew from past experience that if I did get up then I would be blessed and I had also learned that when *He* gets you up, you don't notice any lack of sleep anyway. So I dragged my sleepy body to the bathroom, rinsed my face to wake me, then went down the stairs and promptly began to pray. I prayed ... then I opened the Bible and read a little ... then prayed some more, but I didn't seem to be getting anywhere ... I started to get a bit cross and frustrated. "Lord, what is the point of getting up if I can't hear what You're saying to me? What is it You want to say to me?" Have you ever noticed that even when you may get cross and impatient and you know you don't deserve it, the Lord just ... loves you and speaks tenderly to you ... and you melt? "Rose, when you get up to spend time with Me, it's like re-fuelling the lamp so that you will shine brightly for the rest of the time. You don't necessarily feel or hear anything specific, but you will see a difference at other times. Remember when you were at the Bible College and a group of you had a session of praying in tongues every evening? You didn't feel anything at the time but you saw amazing things happening at other times. Rose, don't you know that sometimes I just want you to sit with Me, and the early morning is the best time for that. Trust Me and you will see. Now let's sit together and watch the sunrise." Which is what He was asking of me in the first place. We don't always have to *do* something; often God just wants us to *be* in Him. '... *to gaze upon the beauty of the LORD and to seek him in his temple.'* You cannot fall in love with someone whom you don't know, so there has to be a desire to know the Lord. In order to know love, open your heart to Jesus, then to show love, open your heart to others and His love will flow through to touch a hurting world. God is love, so the love that is seen as we express it is God. Whoever loves God must also love his brother. While I was leading worship in Leicester on one occasion, as we were singing a chorus, the Lord said to me, "Open your eyes." So I did this and looked out across the people. Then the Lord said, "These are My people and I love them. They are all different from one another. They praise differently, they pray differently, they do things differently, not necessarily wrongly, but differently." Again He said, "These are My people and I love them." As I looked, something seemed to stir within me and went out from my innermost heart to the people. It was the love of God rising up in me. You cannot, and certainly should not, minister to God's people in any way without loving them, not with your love, because there is no good thing in us, so we have no love of our own, but with His love. When we have children, we want them to love us, but we cannot force them to do so. We can only love them and hope that the love will be returned. The choice has to be theirs. In the same way, although we were created for a loving relationship with God, the choice is ours, but there is a cost. We cannot have it without holiness and faith, and all motivation for holiness and faith comes from the loving relationship between ourselves and the Lord. I had been working with a young Muslim man whom I really liked. He was always fasting and praying and he was clearly so hungry for God. We often had some wonderful discussions about the Lord, and one day I was telling him about my conversation during the night. As I spoke, his eyes seemed to get wider and wider and he asked in wonder, "Do you believe that we can connect with God?" "Yes, of course," I said. "That's what I've just been talking about". "Then why did we have prophets?" he asked. So I explained as simply as I could how the prophets were men and women who heard from God for the people, and who also prophesied about the coming of Jesus so that we could have that connection with the Lord. The next time I saw him, I reminded him of our conversation. "Why do you think we were created in the first place?" I asked. "To be obedient, of course," was his quick reply. "No," I said, horrified. "We were created for a *relationship* with God. He *loves* us and wants a family, then *out* of that love relationship with Him, we will obey." He looked at me again, his eyes wide with wonder, and said excitedly, "I want what you've got, I really want it." Hallelujah, Jesus! That's the kind of evangelism I like. That is the difference between 'religion' and being a *true* Christian. (I say *true* Christian because many people call themselves Christians without really knowing what it means.) King David had a growing revelation and understanding of who God is, and also who he (David) was. He saw that the Lord was *almighty* and *sovereign* over all, and without Him, David was nothing. He knew that God's love for him was by grace, undeserved, and yet all that love, protection, guidance and forgiveness were there for him. This was a covenant love relationship and without that love, everything else means nothing. '... *love is the fulfilment of the law.'* Rom.13:10.

'Your love, O LORD, reaches to the heavens, your faithfulness to the skies. Your righteousness is like the mighty mountains, your justice like the great deep. O LORD, you preserve both man and beast. How priceless is your unfailing love! Both high and low among men find refuge in the shadow of your wings. They feast in the abundance of your house; you give them drink from your river of delights. For with you is the fountain of life; in your light we see light.' Psalm 36:5–9.

16

From Beginning To End

Part Five

Whose Power?

"'The time is coming," declares the LORD, "when I will make a new covenant with the house of Israel and with the house of Judah. It will not be like the covenant I made with their forefathers when I took them by the hand to lead them out of Egypt, because they broke my covenant, though I was a husband to them," declares the LORD. "This is the covenant that I will make with the house of Israel after that time," declares the LORD. "I will put my law in their minds and write it on their hearts. I will be their God and they will be my people. ... they will all know me, from the least of them to the greatest," declares the LORD." For I will forgive their wickedness and will remember their sins no more."Jer.31:31–34.

God has revealed to us the importance of these first three covenants being built up in our lives in order that we may know Him, but we have also seen over the whole of the Old Testament how impossible it is to bring this about by ourselves; we need help. The Lord knows this, and so there is a fourth covenant which takes all the plans and promises of the first three covenants and makes them work. This covenant brings the power to make it possible to *know* Him, the power of the cross of Jesus and the power of the Holy Spirit, God's Word and His Spirit working together.Jesus came from heaven to earth to *show* us the way. Through Him, God gives us a whole new start by forgiving and forgetting all our sins, writing His law, His requirement of us, on our hearts, and putting His Holy Spirit *in* us as Ezekiel prophesied.

> *"And I* (the Lord*) will put my Spirit in you and move you to follow my decrees and be careful to keep my laws. You will live in the land I gave your forefathers; you will be my people and I will be your God."*
> Ezek.36:27–28.

God promised that His Spirit would *move* us to follow His ways and keep His law, and He will direct us to the Promised Land where we can truly be His. Jesus came, born of the Spirit yet fully human, born of a virgin and laid in a manger. He grew up in wisdom and stature and favour with God and men, learning the written word and growing as a man in His relationship with His heavenly Father. Even though He was the Son of God, fully God and yet fully man, it was not until after the Holy Spirit descended on Him at the River Jordan that He went out in the anointing of the Spirit, to teach, preach and perform wonders. In the power of the Holy Spirit He walked in the faith, holiness and love which were emphasised in the first three covenants. He came to *fulfil* the Law and the things that were spoken through the prophets.

> *"Do not think that I have come to abolish the Law or the Prophets; I have not come to abolish them but to*

> *fulfil them. I tell you the truth, until heaven and earth*
> *disappear, not the smallest letter, not the least stroke*
> *of a pen, will by any means disappear from the Law*
> *until everything is accomplished."* Matt. 5:17–18.

Jesus fulfilled the Law in the sense that He gave it meaning.
He showed the *real* meaning and principles of the Law and
the need for total commitment *to* it rather than just obedience and knowledge *of* it. He was against legalism and
hypocrisy and keeping the laws externally for show while
breaking them inwardly, as the Pharisees did. They totally
missed the heart of the Law, thinking that righteousness
came through works; whereas Jesus taught that righteousness and the way to God come *only* through faith in *Him* and
His work, by the power of the Holy Spirit.

> *'At that time Jesus came from Nazareth in Galilee and*
> *was baptised by John in the Jordan. As Jesus was*
> *coming up out of the water, he saw heaven being torn*
> *open and the Spirit descending on him like a dove.*
> *And a voice came from heaven: "You are my Son,*
> *whom I love; with you I am well pleased."'* Mark
> 1:9–10.

I often picture this scene in my mind. The Holy Spirit has
been *waiting* for this moment, hovering as He did at the
dawn of creation. As Jesus comes out of the water of
baptism, the Spirit excitedly tears open the heavens crying,
"Yippee! This is it, now things can *really* get going." Then
He zooms in, in the form of a dove so that the Spirit and the
Word could again work together as one as they did in the
beginning. (In the Old Testament, doves were sacrificed as
a poor man's sin offering, and so the Holy Spirit appeared in

the form of a dove to illustrate Jesus as the ultimate sin offering.) And then the Father says, "You are my Son whom I love. I am so pleased with you. Now, as others follow your example and receive the power of my Spirit, they too can become My sons and live as sons of the King. They can be given a brand new start and receive the inheritance which I have planned for them." We know that from this moment Jesus was filled with the Holy Spirit, because immediately afterwards,

'Jesus, full of the Holy Spirit, returned from the Jordan and was led by the Spirit in the desert, where for forty days he was tempted by the devil.' Luke 4:1–2.

He was fully human, living in a fallen world, but by the power of the Holy Spirit and in accordance with the written word of God, the Scriptures, He was able to stand against *all* temptation from the devil. When He left the desert,

'Jesus returned to Galilee in the power of the Spirit, and news about him spread through the whole coun-tryside. He taught in their synagogues, and everyone praised him.' Luke 4:14–15.

Something had changed. There was a new dynamic, and people saw it. Word was getting around and they praised Him.

'He went to Nazareth, where he had been brought up, and on the Sabbath day he went into the synagogue, as was his custom. And he stood up to read. The scroll of the prophet Isaiah was handed to him. Unrolling it, he found the place where it is written: "The Spirit of

the Lord is on me, because he has anointed me to preach good news to the poor. He has sent me to proclaim freedom for the prisoners and recovery of sight for the blind, to release the oppressed, to proclaim the year of the Lord's favour." Then he rolled up the scroll, gave it back to the attendant and sat down. The eyes of everyone in the synagogue were fastened on him, and he began by saying to them, "Today this scripture is fulfilled in your hearing."'
Luke 4:16–21.

It's interesting that Jesus read out a passage declaring that He was anointed to do these things, and then Luke says that He *began* by saying to them, "Today this scripture was fulfilled in your hearing." He believed it, spoke it out and then acted on it. Filled with the Holy Spirit, Jesus was now empowered to heal the sick, cause blind eyes to see, and even to raise the dead. He was able to set people free and to preach and teach with power and authority; – it was time for miracles. For three years, Jesus travelled around performing these miracles, until the day came when, though He was falsely accused, the people rejected Him – and they crucified the King.

'"Here is your King," Pilate said to the Jews. But they shouted, "Take him away! Crucify him!"' John 19:14–15.

He was rejected, bruised and beaten, and took all our sins and pain upon Himself, as was prophesied many years before by Isaiah.

'He was despised and rejected – a man of sorrows, acquainted with bitterest grief. We turned our backs on Him and looked the other way when He went by. He was despised, and we did not care. Yet it was our weaknesses He carried; it was our sorrows that weighed Him down. And we thought His troubles were a punishment from God for His own sins! But He was wounded and crushed for our sins. He was beaten that we might have peace. He was whipped, and we were healed! All of us have strayed away like sheep. We have left God's paths to follow our own. Yet the Lord laid on Him the guilt and sins of us all. He was oppressed and treated harshly, yet He never said a word. He was led like a lamb to the slaughter. And as a sheep is silent before the shearers, He did not open His mouth. From prison and trial they led Him away to His death. But who among the people realised that He was dying for their sins – that He was suffering their punishment? He had done no wrong, and He never deceived anyone. But He was buried like a criminal; He was put in a rich man's grave. But it was the Lord's good plan to crush Him and fill Him with grief. Yet when His life is made an offering for sin, He will have a multitude of children, many heirs. He will enjoy a long life, and the Lord's plan will prosper in His hands. When He sees all that is accomplished by His anguish, He will be satisfied. And because of what He has experienced, My righteous servant will make it possible for many to be counted righteous, for He will bear all their sins.' Isa. 53:3–11. New Living Translation.

Because death could not hold a sinless man, Jesus broke the

curse of death; what Adam had lost, He took back in the power of the Word and Spirit working together.

'When he had received the drink, Jesus said, "It is finished." With that, he bowed his head and gave up his Spirit.' John 19:30.

He said "It is finished" because He had accomplished what He came to do. The veil of the temple was torn in two, the way to God was open; and yet this was a new beginning for mankind – a fresh start. On the third day the Holy Spirit returned to Jesus and God raised His body from death – Jesus is alive! At the Last Supper, before He was betrayed and crucified and knowing what was about to happen, Jesus gave His followers this instruction and promise:

"If you love me, you will obey what I command." (This was something that He knew they would not be able to do in their own strength.) *"And I will ask the Father, and he will give you another counsellor to be with you for ever – the Spirit of truth. The world cannot accept him, because it neither sees him nor knows him. But you know him, for he lives with you and will be in you ... Because I live, you also will live. On that day you will realise that I am in my Father, and you are in me, and I am in you."* John 14:15–20.

The Holy Spirit who had been *with* the disciples *in* Jesus would soon come and live *in them* in the same way as He was *in* Jesus. On the day they received the Holy Spirit to live in *them,* they would realise that Jesus was alive – *in them;* that He and the Father were one, and because His Spirit was in them, they too could be one with God.

'After his suffering, he showed himself to these men (the apostles) and gave many convincing proofs that he was alive. He appeared to them over a period of forty days and spoke about the kingdom of God. On one occasion, while he was eating with them, he gave them this command: "Do not leave Jerusalem, but wait for the gift my Father promised, which you have heard me speak about. For John baptised with water, but in a few days you will be baptised with the Holy Spirit."' Acts 1:3–5.

The same Holy Spirit who had lived in Jesus would come to live in all those who opened their lives to His power. The same things that Jesus had done, His followers would also do, and, in fact, even greater things because now the Holy Spirit would not be limited to one body, but would live in *all* who would receive Him.

"But you will receive power when the Holy Spirit comes on you; and you will be my witnesses in Jerusalem, and in all Judea and Samaria, and to the ends of the earth." Acts 1:8.

This was the last thing that Jesus said to the disciples before He was taken up to Heaven. God the Father had given Him this gift and now He was passing the Spirit on to the church.

"My prayer is not for them alone. I pray also for those who will believe in me through their message, that all of them may be one, Father, just as you are in me and I am in you. May they also be in us so that the world may believe that you have sent me." John 17:20–21.

This means that every church and person who professes to follow Jesus should be experiencing the miracle of Pentecost and the power of the Word and Spirit working through their lives.

'When the day of Pentecost came ... all of them were filled with the Holy Spirit and began to speak in other tongues as the Spirit enabled them.' Acts 2:1–4.

All of them – even Mary, the mother of Jesus. We *all* need the power of the Holy Spirit to live the Christian life. If Jesus needed Him, the disciples needed Him and Mary needed Him, who are we to say we don't? When we are born again, we become a new creation. We have a new beginning, the old life has gone, and Jesus becomes our spiritual husband; the ring is on our finger. When we are baptised in the Holy Spirit, it is like consummating the marriage and we can become 'one' with Him. A man leaves his father and mother and is united to his wife, and they become one flesh. Jesus left His Father to be united with His bride, the church, so that they could become 'one' in Spirit. Jesus gave His life for His bride, but we, as His bride, must also submit our lives to Him.

'[He] is able to do immeasurably more than all we could ask or imagine, according to his power that is at work within us.' Eph. 3:20.

But He can only work with what is in His hands. Many people invite Jesus into their lives and are saved, but they have not *given* their lives to *Him*. They may even have been baptised in the Spirit but they have not really submitted themselves completely, instead preferring to stay in control of their own lives. Then they wonder why this Christian life is not working for them. A seed has to fall to the ground and die to produce a harvest. If we want to really know our King and to have an intimate relationship with Him, if we want move into the fullness of His plan for us and to build the temple to contain the glory, then it has to be His way, not ours. We have to allow Him to guide us in every situation, *dying* to our own will and realising that it *has* to be *Him*, not me, and this is an ongoing battle. Even the Apostle Paul struggled with this issue.

I praise God that He takes the weak things and raises them up to show His glory, because apart from Him we can do nothing. We don't even know how to pray without the Holy Spirit interceding. The sooner we realise, as Paul did, that there really is no good thing in us, and hand everything over for the Lord to do, the more we will start to see the fruit in our lives.

'"Not by might nor by power, but by my Spirit," says the LORD Almighty.' Zech. 4:6.

I was so excited when I was invited to preach in the church where I had been saved and baptised. I truly wanted to bless them and encourage them in their relationship with Jesus. Then only a few days before I was due to go, I sat at my dressing table, thinking, "I've had three months to prepare a word for this meeting and I still haven't done anything … Maybe the Lord doesn't want me to prepare anything. After all, He has been teaching me recently about trusting Him more." These thoughts then flowed into actual speech to the Lord, "But Lord, this one is *so* special, it's so important that I have the right word for them, and I really *do* want to encourage them. I *must* get something together for it." His

148

reply came quickly, "Oh, I see, you mean it's too important for Me to do, do you?" Ouch! I asked for that one. I didn't dare prepare anything then, apart from handing it all over to Him and choosing to trust Him. And guess what? It *was* special and it *did* encourage the people; in fact it did everything *He* wanted it to, because it was done in *His* power and not in mine. Praise His wonderful Name!

17

From Beginning To End

Part Six

It's the Vision

Four covenants between God and Man, running right through the Bible and covering the whole of time. They highlight the four pillars of the temple that need to be built up in our lives: Faith, Holiness, Love and Power. However, I was confused. "Lord, our church pastor taught us that the four pillars were first Holiness, then Faith, followed by Love and Power, but what You have shown *me* is *Faith* first, *then* Holiness. Why are they in a different order? Have I heard You wrongly?" "No," was His reply. "Colin was teaching from the New Testament, but what I have shown you begins in the Old Testament and continues into the New. Colin's teaching was about believers *after* Jesus had come to earth and been crucified and had risen again. These people are already saved, so holiness comes first. But because the teaching I gave you dates from Old Testament times, it was necessary for faith to come first." "Oh, I see!" I said, as revelation dawned. Then I asked another question, "Lord, what about the foundations of the temple? Pastor Colin taught that we must have firm foundations to build on, and spoke of three layers, all found in Jesus and what He has done. The first layer is revelation of the cross and what You have already accomplished through Jesus, when He died to make the way for us. The second layer is revelation of our position *in* Christ, of who we are in Him, seated in heavenly places, and the third layer is revelation of what we have inherited through Jesus, eternal life with Him. So what are the grounds for what You have shown me?"

I didn't hear the answer immediately, but next morning I woke up hearing the words, "It's the vision.""The vision?" I asked. "What do you mean, Lord? I don't understand ... what vision?" Again I didn't immediately hear the answer, but the following day I woke with a verse of Scripture on my mind:

> *'In the beginning was the Word, and the Word was with God, and the Word was God. He was with God in the beginning. Through him all things were made; without him nothing was made that has been made.'* John 1:1–3.

"Of course!" I said excitedly as the meaning hit me. "That's it!" Jesus was there in the beginning; through Him all things were made. He was *there* in Eden. Eden was a *picture* of what God *planned* for mankind, and that means the Garden of Eden was the *'vision,'* – that we should walk and talk with Him, be in intimate relationship with Him, and be totally dependent upon Him. We live in time, but with God there is *no* time, for He dwells in eternity, which is outside and beyond time. He is the beginning *and* the end, the Alpha and the Omega. He knows the beginning from the end because He sees it all now, and it's *all* in His hands. The foundations of the temple that the Lord was showing me were exactly the same as He showed Colin. The first layer is the cross of Jesus. It is very difficult for us to grasp, but in God's eyes, Jesus' death and resurrection had already happened when

Adam and Eve lived in the Garden of Eden. It was His plan that Jesus would make the way for us to be reconciled to God. We can only see it in the perspective of time and space, but God sees it from the perspective of eternity. It was a 'done' deal! The second layer of the temple foundation is still our position in Christ. We were chosen before the beginning of time, before the creation of the world, to be set apart for Him as God's sons. Our position as believers has *always* been that we are seated with Him in heavenly places. The third layer of this heavenly temple is our inheritance in Jesus, "Eden life", fullness of life.

> *"I have come that they may have life, and have it to the full."* John 10:10.

It's eternal life, every spiritual blessing, health, provision, peace and joy, in fact, everything that Adam and Eve had in the Garden of Eden before the fall. We are called to be holy and blameless in God's sight. It's all ours in Him even now – by faith.

> *'For no-one can lay any foundation other than the one already laid, which is Jesus Christ.'* 1 Cor. 3:11.

In God's sight, it was *already* laid when time began. He is Lord of time and eternity.

Yes, God *is* building His temple where His glory and goodness may be made manifest and where He can live with His people, a place where the bride and her King can live in intimacy. We are in the last days, time is short and we need to be ready. God is building His church. As the song goes,

'For I'm building a people of power,
And I'm making a people of praise,
That will move through this land
(this world) *by My Spirit*
And will glorify My precious Name.'

D.Richards, Copyright 1977
Thankyou Music, Eastbourne

He is building and there is no greater time than now for God's people to come to know Him and to move out in the Spirit to glorify His Name. But –

"... Unless a grain of wheat falls to the ground and dies, it remains only a single seed. But if it dies, it produces many seeds. The man who loves his life will lose it, while the man who hates his life in this world will keep it for eternal life. Whoever serves me must follow me; and where I am, my servant also will be."
John 12:24–26.

Jesus was the Son of God who died to produce many sons for God, so if we profess to follow and serve Jesus, then we will also follow Him to death. To build the temple and to live as His bride means to surrender our will to His, to *die.* It is no longer I who live, but Christ who lives in me. One day, not long before Gerry and I were married, we had a big argument. I can't remember what it was about and it's not important now, but I do remember at one point suddenly hearing my own voice scream out, "I don't want to die!" I was shocked. Wow! Where did that come from? ... Then I realised what the argument had *really* been about. I was having an identity crisis and desperately trying to hold on to my life. When a woman marries a man, she gives up her own name and takes on that of her husband. My name had been important to me; I had my own business, "Rose White Display", my own home and my own life. When I was in my early twenties, I used to say that I didn't want to be a nobody, I wanted to be a somebody, and now suddenly I felt as though I were disappearing. I felt as if I was becoming just an extension of Gerry, an accessory, and I wasn't even going to have my own name any more. Of course, Satan encouraged these thoughts, as he does if we let him. The argument was really about me staying in control of my life, wanting to be noticed and accepted, to be a somebody. I didn't want to die ... Now I realise that without the Lord, I *am* nothing, there is *no* good thing in me. How dare I even consider that I could be something special without Him and apart from what He makes me? He is the Almighty Creator of the heavens and the earth and He alone deserves the glory. Stubbornness and pride will only serve to keep us out of His presence, and so unless I am broken, He cannot use me. I am simply a clay pot, although one which contains the treasure of Jesus, but unless the pot is broken, the treasure cannot be revealed. When Isaiah saw the Lord (Isaiah chapter six), he saw that he was a man of unclean lips who lived among a people of unclean lips. In other words, he saw how immense God is and how small he was. He was broken of self. The greater the revelation of our Lord, the more you see your nothingness, and yet He loves us in spite of the rubbish in our lives. In Him I have everything, and with Him nothing is impossible. If you are going through a time of seeing the dirt in your life, be encouraged, as this is drawing you closer to the Lord. The bride has to lose her own identity and take on a new name. As a Christian, I take the Name and life of Jesus, in whom I am totally accepted. In Him, I *am* a 'somebody', the precious child of the King, not just any king but the King of kings. When I married Gerry, I didn't *lose* my identity; I *found* it, because I was in the will of God. I am the bride of Christ, as also is Gerry, so we *both* take on His new name together. The old King had to die before Isaiah saw the Lord (Isaiah 6:1)

> *'Your attitude should be the same as that of Christ Jesus: Who, being in very nature God, did not consider equality with God something to be grasped, but made himself nothing, taking the very nature of a servant, being made in human likeness. And being found in appearance as a man, he humbled himself and became obedient to death – even death on a cross! Therefore God exalted him to the highest place and gave him the name that is above every name, that at the name of Jesus every knee should bow, in heaven and on earth and under the earth, and every tongue confess that Jesus Christ is Lord, to the glory of God the Father.'* Phil. 2:5–11.

Every created being will confess that Jesus Christ is *Lord*. In the period of time just before I went to YWAM, before I knew anything about going, I regularly attended an early morning prayer meeting in our church. On one particular morning the idea came to me that I was to wash everyone's feet. I thought I must have heard wrongly; or at least I hoped that I had heard wrongly and it certainly wasn't the most appealing idea that I could have come up with. The pastor agreed that I should go for it, and so with a towel on my knee, a bowl of warm water and some soap, the prayer people all went home with cleaner feet than they had arrived with. (Especially one young man, bless him!) It was a very embarrassing and humbling exercise both for me and for them, and it wasn't until years later that I realised what it was all about. The Lord was testing me: was I willing to serve others, even when it was uncomfortable and I didn't understand? Was I willing to die to pride and embarrassment to follow Jesus' example? I often wonder if He would still have taken me to YWAM and onwards if I had not been obedient on this occasion, and I praise God that I had a pastor who listened to the Holy Spirit. A definition of a good Christian, a follower of Christ, is someone who is willing to die. Revival comes out of brokenness of 'self', demonstrating submission to go with Him wherever He leads. One day, the Lord showed me a picture of two people walking along a path in a wood or forest. They were so deep in conversation that they never noticed anything around them. Suddenly they found themselves in a beautiful clearing, where one of them gasped in wonder, saying, "This is amazing! How did we get here?" The Lord told me that this is how the work that He had been doing through us in Uganda came about. We were just walking, so engrossed in Him that we never noticed where He was taking us, then suddenly, we looked at the buildings of the Bible College and the Job Skills Training Centre springing up and thought, "Lord, how did all this happen?" You see, we never planned any of it. We just walked where He led and did what He told us to do, and He brought it all into being around us. We cannot take the credit for anything, it's all His. The challenge now, of course, is to stay in that place of simply walking with the Lord and not try to take over from Him. I know that if we do interfere, we will certainly get in the way and lose God's best both for ourselves *and* for the people over there.

To move into the fullness of the 'vision' of God, His best, we have to die to what we want. The 'flesh' must go. When

Paul prayed for the thorn in his side to be removed, it wasn't so much the thorn that was the problem; it was the flesh into which it was sticking. God said, "My grace is sufficient." He will enable us to overcome as we submit to Him. The vision that God has given to us of "Eden life" through Jesus is the foundation that will sustain and encourage us, knowing that He is the Sovereign King and that nothing is hidden from Him or is outside His Lordship.

18

The East Gate

I believe that God's purpose throughout the whole of time has been to create His children. We are saved, are now being saved and will continue to be saved. All through time, He has been shaping and forming us into His image, in preparation for the vision that He revealed to us in the beginning. He has been preparing a bride for Jesus, a bride who is dressed in white.

> *'God saw all that he had made, and it was very good. And there was evening, and there was morning – the sixth day. Thus the heavens and the earth were completed in all their vast array. By the seventh day God had finished the work he had been doing; so on the seventh day he rested from all his work.'* Gen. 1:31–2:2.

God rested on the seventh day because the work was finished, and as was said in chapter twelve of this book, all He had to do then was to sit back and wait for the process of time to take its course. Creation itself had to now take its course according to the predestined plan and purpose of God's will, and so it is our responsibility to follow that plan and be a part of it.First of all, Adam and Eve tasted "Eden life", fullness of life, walking with the Lord – they saw the vision. Eve was deceived and then Adam chose to disobey God, resulting in their separation from Him and a life of pain, fear, hardship

159

and death, no longer clothed in God's glory, but instead clothed in the skins of animals. The whole earth was cursed because Adam and Eve chose to do what *they* wanted instead of what God had said. God is holy and cannot look upon sin, so for *our* sake they *had* to be banished from the Garden. They *had* to be separated from the Tree of Life, otherwise mankind would have had no choice but to live forever in this fallen state, not because it was God's will, but because it was the consequence of man's disobedience and independence.

> *'And the LORD God said, "The man has now become like one of us, knowing good and evil. He must not be allowed to reach out his hand and take also from the tree of life and eat, and live for ever." So the LORD God banished him from the Garden of Eden to work the ground from which he had been taken. After he drove the man out, he placed on the east side of the Garden of Eden cherubim and a flaming sword flashing back and forth to guard the way to the tree of life.'* Gen.3:22–24.

The east gate was closed and locked, and throughout the thousands of years that have passed since then, God has been teaching and shaping us, preparing and showing us the right way to Him, while man has been trying to do it himself and failing over and over again. In the tenth chapter of Ezekiel, the prophet speaks about the glory of God leaving the temple because of sin. In chapter forty-three, he has a vision of the glory returning from the east, entering through the *east gate* and filling the temple once again. The temple becomes the place of God's throne, where He will live with His people for ever, on condition that they put aside everything else and turn back to Him.

"Now let them put away from me their prostitution and the lifeless idols of their kings, and I will live among them for ever. Son of man, describe the temple to the people of Israel, (God's people), *that they may be ashamed of their sins. Let them consider the plan, and if they are ashamed of all they have done,* (if they have the desire to get their lives right with God), *make known to them the design of the temple – its arrangement, its exits and entrances* (the things that will take you out of the presence of God and the things that will enable you to enter before Him) *–its whole design and all its regulations and laws.* (what God requires of us). *Write these down before them so that they may be faithful to its design and follow all its regulations."* Ezek. 43:9–11.

This is what I have attempted to do in this book.

We have this promise that the relationship with the Lord *will* be restored and the glory of God will again fill the temple, but we also know that the east gate is closed and guarded.

'Then the man brought me back to the outer gate of the sanctuary, the one facing, east, and it was shut. The LORD said to me, "This gate is to remain shut. It must not be opened; no-one may enter through it. It is to remain shut because the LORD, the God of Israel, has entered through it. The prince himself is the only one who may sit inside the gateway to eat in the presence of the LORD."' Ezek. 44 1–3.

The glory of the Lord was believed to be present in the Holy of Holies in the temple, but only the High Priest could enter there, and then only once a year. The Bible tells us that Jesus is our great High Priest for ever, and this means that He is our only hope.

'Therefore, since we have a great high priest who has gone through the heavens, Jesus the Son of God, let us hold firmly to the faith we profess.' Heb.4:14.

Jesus is the Prince Himself, and is the *only* one who can go through the east gate and have fellowship and eat with the Father, so unless *He* opens the gate we have no way of ever returning to "Eden life" or to a relationship with God.

When Jesus was crucified on the cross at Golgotha, He cried out in a loud voice and gave up His spirit.

'At that moment the curtain of the temple was torn in two from top to bottom.' Matt. 27:51.

This symbolised that the way into the presence of God was now open; the way into the temple was through the *east* gate.

'Therefore, brothers, since we have confidence to enter the Most Holy Place by the blood of Jesus, by a new and living way opened for us through the curtain, that is, his body and since we have a great priest over the house of God, let us draw near to God with a sincere heart in full assurance of faith, having our hearts sprinkled to cleanse us from a guilty conscience and having our bodies washed with pure water. Let us hold unswervingly to the hope we profess, for he who promised is faithful.' Heb. 10:19–23.

Through His death on the cross, Jesus opened the way to God.But now let me show you something more. In John's Gospel, after Jesus had cried out, *"It is finished,"* and given up His spirit, we read,

> *'Now it was the day of Preparation, and the next day was to be a special Sabbath. Because the Jews did not want the bodies left on the crosses during the Sabbath, they asked Pilate to have the legs broken and the bodies taken down. The soldiers therefore came and broke the legs of the first man who had been crucified with Jesus, and then those of the other. But when they came to Jesus and found that he was already dead, they did not break his legs. Instead, one of the soldiers pierced Jesus' side with a spear, bringing a sudden flow of blood and water.'* John 19:31–34.

Why did they pierce His side? We know that His legs were not broken, in order to fulfil what was prophesied in Scripture, but why pierce His side? The answer is that primarily, the soldiers wanted to make sure that Jesus really was dead, as He had died in less time than normal. This makes it clear that He had laid down His life of His own accord and it was not taken from Him. The spear was thrust into His side to His heart, and so must have entered on His left side. Imagine Jesus as He hung on the cross. As you are facing Him, above his head is 'north', below His feet is 'south', to His right is west, leaving the side that was pierced to be the … *'east'*. His side was pierced to open the gate, the east gate, to all who will believe. As the soldier pierced Jesus' side with the spear, there was a sudden flow of blood and water, symbolising blood for atonement and water for purification. The river of God flows from the temple and where the river flows there is life. Jesus is the temple, so the same river that flowed in the Garden of Eden to water and bring life was flowing again through Him. Jesus spoke of living waters to the woman at the well: " ... *whoever drinks the water I give him will never thirst. Indeed, the water I give him will become in him a spring of water welling up to eternal life."* John 4:.14. The east gate is open and we can go right in.

> *"A time is coming and has now come when the true worshippers will worship the Father in spirit and truth, for they are the kind of worshippers the Father seeks. God is spirit, and his worshippers must worship in spirit and truth."* John 4:23–24.

We can only do that as we drink of the living waters, as we step through the east gate into the flow of His life, which comes straight from His heart. In chapter twelve, I referred to the creation of man and woman as a picture of the gospel message. Eve, the rib, was taken from Adam's side and then they were put back together to be 'one' in marriage. Possibly, the rib was taken from the left side closest to Adam's heart. Do you see the connection? – Mankind was taken from the glory and presence of God, from being close to His heart, and now, in the course of time, can be made one again with Him as the bride of Christ. In each case, – of Adam's rib, Ezekiel's vision and the Garden of Eden, the opening was closed and sealed. The woman is by nature the 'doorway to life', meaning that new birth comes through her body and she bears children, so the river that flows from the east gate of the temple is to flow *through* the bride of Christ. And where the river flows, there is life.

I was on my knees in worship with my arms held up and

out and my head bowed. The presence of the Lord was so strong that I could neither move nor speak. As I bowed before the throne of God, I saw, not *myself* with my hands stretched out and head bowed, but *Jesus* on the cross. I was looking at Him from above His head, as His Father would have done if He had been able to bear to look. I saw His hair matted with blood from wounds caused by the sharp thorns of the crown that was on His head. There were ropes tied tightly round His wrists to the rough wood of the cross and the blood was beginning to dry from the wounds on His hands where the vicious nails were hammered in. I couldn't quite see the wound in His side from where the spear had pieced Him, but I saw the blood and water gushing from His side. Suddenly, I saw that it wasn't Jesus on that cross, it was *me*, – it *was* Jesus, and yet it was it was also *me*. My hair, too, was matted with blood from the crown of thorns; my hands, too, were bound and sticky with blood from the nails. I had been crucified *with* Him. Now the river of life that was flowing from *His* side was flowing from *mine*. The east gate of the temple of God, the way to intimacy and knowledge of the King, was opened up so that the river of life could flow out. Because my side too was pierced, the river could also now flow through me, from Jesus' heart in me to a hurting world. As I get to know my King, focusing more on Him and less on myself, and gain more understanding and revelation of what it is that I have within me, that life will flow more and more freely through me, and others will be drawn in through the east gate to know Jesus for themselves.

The Bible says: *'He who believes in me, as the scripture has said, out of his heart will flow rivers of living water.'* John 7:38.NKJ.

The life, love and Spirit of Jesus indwell me. I sat down one day with my pencils and sketchpad, following an urge to copy a small picture that I had found of the face of Jesus. As I began, I said, "Lord, this is my worship to You," for no other reason than that it seemed a good thing to say, and I *did* want to bless Him. I didn't find it easy at first and cried out in frustration, "Lord, help me, I'm losing it," and then I heard, "No, you're not. Keep going, keep going." The nose I had drawn seemed too small for a Jewish man's nose, but for some reason, hard as I tried, I couldn't change the shape, so I left it as it was. After two or three hours, I looked at the finished drawing and was delighted, hardly believing that I had done it. Praise God! I stood the drawing on the mantelpiece where I could see it to check for any faults there might be, but every time I looked, somehow it reminded me of someone, apart from the obvious, that is. Then I started to think that it reminded me of – *myself,* which was ridiculous. Even so, I looked in the mirror and then at the drawing; I fetched a photograph to compare, but decided. "No, I'm imagining it." Putting the drawing back on the shelf, I walked towards the kitchen and suddenly it was as though a light came on – I remembered what I had been asking God: "Lord, how do you see me?" I went back to the drawing, put one piece of paper over the forehead, another over the mouth, and guess what? Yes, it was a picture of me. It was a mirror image, what I saw when I looked in the mirror. One eye was slightly higher and bigger than the other as mine were, the cheekbones were mine, and the reason that I couldn't change the nose was because it was my nose. My daughter said that the mouth was also mine, but of course there were a beard and moustache on the drawing. It was amazing. When I asked the Lord how He saw me, this was His answer. He was saying, "When I look at you, I see Jesus, Jesus *in* you." I am in Jesus and He is in me. We cannot be separated. Where He goes, I go, and where I go, He goes too. I have been crucified with Him; the old life is finished, so as I surrender my life to Him, His life becomes mine. I am the only Jesus that many people in the world will see, as are you. What do they see? Is the river flowing from *your* life? Is the east gate open through you? In John's Gospel again, we read about when Jesus appeared to Thomas. After His resurrection, Jesus had already appeared to the other disciples, but Thomas doubted the truth of their testimony that they had seen Jesus.

> *'But he said to them, "Unless I see the nail marks in his hands and put my finger where the nails were, and put my hand into his side, I will not believe it." A* week *later ... though the doors were locked, Jesus came and stood among them, and said ... to Thomas, "Put your finger here; see my hands. Reach out your hand and put it into my side. Stop doubting and believe."'* John 20:25 – 27.

See the truth of what Jesus did for you on the cross, reach out and grasp it, *choose* to believe and then you will see. Unlock the door of unbelief that is blocking the way. After this, *'Thomas said to him, "My Lord and my God!"'* Thomas had received revelation of the risen Christ, the *Lord*, the Son of God. Continuing the story from verse thirty, we read,

> *"Jesus did many other miraculous signs in the presence of his disciples, which are not recorded in this book. But these are written that you may believe that Jesus is the Christ, the Son of God, and that by believing you may have life in his name."*

The preceding passages are all about people *seeing* the risen *Lord* Jesus, really seeing and believing, and the first of these was a woman. This revelation brings *life*:

> "… *and on this rock* (revelation that Jesus is *Lord*) *I will build my church, and the gates of Hades will not overcome it."* Matt. 16:18.

The east gate is open, and when you reach out and touch the life flow of the Lord, as Thomas was instructed to do, you cannot fail to receive revelation of who He is and of who you are in Him, so that His life can flow through you.In Revelation chapter twenty-one, John's vision of the new Jerusalem, the Holy City, where we are to live with our God and He will live with us, we read in verse twenty-five, *'On no day will its gates ever be shut …'* And Rev. 22:14 reads:

> "*Blessed are those who wash their robes* (in the blood of Jesus), *that they may have the right to the tree of life and may go through the gates into the city."*

… back into "Eden life", only better, because now we know what we are choosing. Child of God, this is not just for the future; the east gate is open *now* for you to live in heavenly places, and it will *never* close again. The sword that stood between man and *Life* at the entrance to the Garden of Eden, has been turned around to form a cross to form a bridge. What God opens, no-one can shut.

19

Because He Loves Me

'For God so loved the world that he gave his one and only Son, that whoever believes in him shall not perish but have eternal life. For God did not send his Son into the world to condemn the world, but to save the world through him.' John 3:16 and 17.

'Through him' – The love of God comes through Jesus. Because He first loved me, I can love Him. Because He first loved me, I can love others. When we were still sinners, He came to save us. We did not and could not get ourselves right with God before Jesus came; that's why we needed a Saviour. We are totally dependent on His love for us. The things that I have spoken of in this book can only come through dependence on *Him* and *His love*; when the Lord said to me, "Rose, just love Me," even that I could not do on my own. What He was really saying was, "Rose, I love you. Receive this, believe it, and then you will begin to know and understand who you are to Me and live in the benefits of it. Because I love you, you can love Me, and everything else will flow from that." The more I understand of His love for me, the easier it will be to follow and serve Him. Only faith pleases God, and you can only trust someone whom you know loves you and has in mind the best for you. Many people believe *in* Jesus, believe that He is real and *there*, but they find it difficult to believe that He is *here with them*, and that He

cares about them personally. Love comes from relationship. The closer you walk with the Lord, the more dependent upon Him and trustful you will be. Time is short and Jesus is coming back soon, so there is no better time than now to draw nearer to God as the whole earth groans with the weight of sin and death. Revival, greater than the world has ever known before, is coming and Jesus is calling His children to come closer both to Him and to each other, so that the world will see. All over the earth, He is saying the same things, preparing His people for this mighty move of the Spirit, and there is a growing expectancy that something is happening. Recently, while in Uganda, the Lord gave me a prophetic word, and I have since realised that it links in with what He's been saying here in England, in Malta and even Australia, and I'm sure also in many other countries as well. Hear what He says to you through this word.

'My lover spoke and said to me, "Arise, my darling, my beautiful one, and come with me. See! The winter is past; the rains are over and gone. Flowers appear on the earth; the season of singing has come, the cooing of doves is heard in our land. The fig-tree forms its early fruit; the blossoming vines spread their fragrance. Arise, come, my darling; my beautiful one, come with me." Song of Songs 2:10–13.

The Lord is calling His beautiful bride to arise and come closer. He's calling you and me to arise *today – now*. This is a new day, a new season. The winter is past; yesterday has gone, so let go of it and move on to a new season of God's favour and grace, where believers will be accelerated into another dimension in the Spirit. *'The rains are over and gone.'* – The rainy season should have long gone when I first spoke out this word in Uganda, but as I spoke, as if to confirm the word, the rain suddenly stopped. Circumstances may try to fool you into thinking that nothing has changed, that the season is still the same, but don't be fooled by circumstances. Look at what God says in His word, only He is the Truth.

'*Flowers appear on the earth.*'- This is to be a season when believers will blossom in their love relationship with Jesus as they hunger and thirst for something deeper, no longer satisfied with where they are but wanting to grow, like flowers coming into full bloom, growing strong and tall and beautiful, as they reach out for more of the sun, and spreading the fragrant aroma of Christ wherever they are. '*The season of singing has come.*'– This will be a time when our lives will be a love song to Jesus. We won't just be *singing* love songs *to* Him, but our whole life will be that expression of love for Him, a love song to the bridegroom. Worship to the Lord will be our lifestyle.'*The cooing of doves is heard in the land'.* – The dove represents a number of things. Firstly, it represents love. As the children of God move into a deeper intimacy with Jesus and begin to understand His love for them, that love will flow through them, to one another and to the world, like a river flowing, bringing life, healing, restoration and freedom wherever it goes. We *are* the river of God when we believe. The second thing that the dove represents is peace. In these difficult times of war and strife, it's hard to understand how we can have peace, but *this* peace is a peace that passes all understanding. When Jesus went back to be with His Father, He sat down because the work was done. As we draw near to our King, we sit down with Him on the mercy seat. Seated with Him in heavenly places, we have peace in the midst of our circumstances. This is the Sabbath-rest, where we don't need to constantly feel we have to 'do', but where we can just 'be' in Him, *knowing* that He is in control, that He is sovereign over all. Thirdly, the dove represents the Holy Spirit. When Jesus was baptised, the Holy Spirit descended on Him in the form of a dove bringing the power of God, His Word and His Spirit working together. Instead of simply hearing the Word, we will be *living* it in the power of the Holy Spirit, and signs and wonders will follow the preaching of the Word in greater measure than we've known before. Lastly, the dove is a symbol of sacrifice. Jesus, the ultimate sacrifice, gave His life for us, and we are called to follow His example. This move of God will bring a greater surrendering of people's lives to be given over for God's purposes. They will be broken of self-dependence, and will realise that in them there really is nothing good, that without God they can do absolutely nothing of any consequence.

> *'The sacrifices of God are a broken spirit; a broken and contrite heart ...'* Ps. 51:17.

Revival comes out of brokenness, humility and dependence on God. His Spirit will flow through the land, in you and me, as our lives are surrendered to Him as living sacrifices. *'The fig-tree forms its early fruit.'* – As the love relationship between Jesus and His bride, the church, grows, then the fruit of new birth will come to many. As our lives influence the lost, we will reap a harvest of souls who are attracted to what they see.

This reminds me of another vision when I saw a big ornate chair. "Oh, is that my throne?" I asked, almost with tongue in cheek, not really expecting it to be. Then a voice said, "Get in and sit down." ... Although this took me by surprise, I did as requested, but was even more surprised when poles were inserted into rings on the sides of the chair and I was lifted up. I looked around me in a daze and was amazed to see a *huge* procession of people following, as far as the eye could see. "I don't understand," I said bewildered. "Who are all these people?" And the Lord said, "These are all the people whom you have influenced during your life. Sometimes just a smile, sometimes something you did or said, or even the way you lived. Most times you didn't even know." People are watching us all the time. What are they seeing and hearing? Lord, let it be good fruit. '... *the blossoming vines spread their fragrance.*' – As the children of God are blossoming and spreading the fragrance of Jesus, the fruit comes and then *they* spread *their* fragrance, bringing multiplication. God wants us to know Him in a way that will reproduce His character, and *His* heart is for the lost, '... *not wanting anyone to perish, but everyone to come to repentance.*' 2 Pet. 3:9. '*Arise my darling; my beautiful one, come with me.*' – You are His beloved, His bride, His beautiful creation that was *so very good.* The King loves you with a passion, so don't just invite Him into your life, *give* yourself to Him, wholly and completely. He can only work with what is in His hands and He can only bless you with the fullness of His life if you go with Him. This passage in the Song of Songs goes on: –

> '*My dove in the clefts of the rock, in the hiding places on the mountainside, show me your face, let me hear your voice; for your voice is sweet and your face is lovely.*'

Jesus is the rock in whom we are placed; He is our hiding place where we '*rest in the shadow of the Almighty.*' Safe in His arms! '*My dove,*' – my love. Our King loves to see your face and hear your voice when you come to Him in praise and worship and He misses you when you are not there. On our most recent trip to Uganda, the room where we were sleeping at the training centre in Kiyindi was very close to the worship hall. Every morning before it was light, Pastor Dan, his family and others in the church would get up to spend very loud prayer times with the Lord. Because the mosquitoes are the most active at that time, (and they *love* the taste of me), we didn't always join them in the hall, but would stay under the net in our beds and join in the prayer from there. It was actually difficult to do anything else because of the volume of prayer in the hall, and also if we joined them, a translator would be needed. One morning as I lay there listening, trying unsuccessfully to distinguish the different voices, in the midst of the noise I became aware of a bird singing, then another bird. It was beautiful. The Lord told me that He hears every individual voice, and He notices and misses us when we don't come. Each voice is a beautiful sound to Him and He loves to see each face looking up to Him. This is how He sees our relationship with Him. If all this is too "romantic" for you, then you'll need to get used to it because we're talking about Revival here. God has said it will happen and what He has said will surely come to pass! Revival is definitely coming – but watch out, for there will be a cost, as other areas of our lives will be affected.

'*Catch for us the little foxes, the little foxes that ruin the vineyard, our vineyards that are in bloom.*' When God moves and the people begin to rise up and bloom, the enemy will also rise bringing distractions, persecution, pride and many other worldly influences. Watch out for the things that will try to creep in to spoil your relationship with God, and get rid of them.

Following this prophetic word in reference to catching the little foxes, the Lord directed me to the book of Revelation, to the letters to the seven churches found in chapters two and three. In each of these letters, the Lord reveals to the churches the 'little foxes' that were ruining, or could potentially ruin, the vineyard and their relationship with Him. Each warning is followed by a number of promises to those who overcame these things, which means to be restored to a right relationship with God. The church at Ephesus had started off well and was very loyal in many ways, but their loyalty had become more for the church than for the Lord. Their attention had been diverted from Christ to the works they were doing for Him, and they had lost sight of their love relationship with Him – the "little fox" of losing their first love and slipping into religion. The answer for them, as it also is for us when we begin to backslide and slip into routine, was simply to repent and turn back to God. If they overcame in this, they could come straight back into that love relationship and live with Him in it.

There had been much suffering and poverty in the church at Smyrna and they were about to go through a time of persecution. To them the Lord gave a warning not to let the "little fox" of fear come in, and to be faithful even if it meant physical death. If they overcame in this they would receive the crown of *Life*, the winner's crown, eternal life with Jesus. God's word to you, whatever you are going through is:

"Be strong and courageous. Do not be afraid or terrified because of them, for the LORD your God goes with you; he will never leave you nor forsake you." Deut. 31:6.

He *is* with you and has *not* given you a spirit of fear. He is greater than your situation, so refuse to accept the fear and *choose* to trust Him. – You *can* do it.

The Lord knew that the church at Pergamum was situated in a difficult area dominated by Satan, but He was pleased that they had remained faithful even in times of persecution.

175

However, they were also tolerating and turning a blind eye to sin in the church. To continue as they were would bring judgment on them, whereas to overcome these "foxes" would result in their receiving hidden manna (revelation and understanding of the truth in the Word) and a white stone with a new name written on it. (The bride of Christ takes on His Name and authority.) The Lord knows and understands that we live in a fallen world, surrounded by evil and worldly influences, but to tolerate these things in the life of the church could only result in destruction. Repentance means that the Lord can take you onwards and upwards.The church at Thyatira was another church which was doing well in many ways, with many good deeds, love and faithfulness, but they were in compromise, tolerating a false prophet who was misleading some of the people. Little foxes will eventually become big foxes if they are left to run freely. If the church overcame these things, they would be given authority over the nations and all the works of the enemy, just as Jesus was given. They would also receive the morning star, which means that from that time on, the evil that is hidden in the dark would be revealed to them in the light of the truth of Jesus. It is vitally important that we learn Scripture for ourselves so that we will not be deceived by false teaching and in order that we may take authority over the devil's schemes. The church in Sardis was known as an 'on fire' church, but in reality was superficial with no real depth. Most, although not all of them were just going through the motions of being Christians, having no genuine relationship with the Lord. They knew His Word but there was no Life. The Lord was saying, "'Wake up before it's too late. My Word needs to move from your heads to your hearts, so that you can live in its truth." If they overcame these things, they would be dressed in white as the bride of Christ and belong to Jesus for ever. Look at your own relationship with Jesus, have you slipped into superficiality? If you have then this is the time for you too to wake up before it's too late. I love the church in Philadelphia, because they had an open door to the presence of God. They knew their own weakness, but in the Lord's strength had kept His Word and been obedient to His commands. Because of their faith and devotion to God, people who were entrapped in religion would see and be drawn to the life in them. If they held on to what they had and overcame any "little foxes" that might try to spoil this relationship with God, no weapon that was forged against them would prosper. They would be made a pillar in the temple of God, for ever before His throne. They would be known as children of God, because they lived in Jesus' Name and strength. It takes regular exercise to keep muscles strong, and in the same way, it takes daily devotion to maintain our marriage relationship with Jesus.

The last of the seven churches was in Laodicea, where the people were lukewarm in their relationship with God, neither hot nor cold. They were comfortable in their lives and didn't see the need for Jesus – putting their trust in themselves and their possessions and money. They were proud, deceived and blind, thinking that their wealth was a sign of spiritual blessings. The Lord was knocking on the door of their hearts and saying, "Let me in, let me in to every part of your life so that we can be together." If you overcome these "foxes" that prevent you from opening the door to Jesus and seeing your life filled with the treasures of heaven, you can sit with Jesus on the throne, as a co-heir to the Kingdom of God and a bride for the King. Putting other things before God will only serve to block your view, causing you to lose sight of your relationship with Jesus.

To every one of these churches, these words were spoken: "He who has an ear, let him hear what the Spirit says to the churches." Are you listening to what He is saying? Can you hear Him? Are you close enough to hear that still small voice saying,

"This is the way, walk in it"? Are you close enough to hear His heartbeat for the nations and the longing in His heart for you? Are you willing to listen and obey even when He points out the "little foxes" that you want to hold on to? Are you listening to the words of love spoken by the bridegroom for His bride? He is saying, "Arise my darling; my beautiful one, come with me." The choice is yours, you can either stay on the outside, still saved but just looking from a distance, or you can join with us to go higher and deeper and further with the King of kings.

God is moving in a powerful way these days, to stir up the hearts of His people for a more intimate knowledge of Him. Out of this will come a holy passion for Jesus such as we've never known before. Because He first loved us, we can love Him, but *only* as we receive revelation of His love for us. We will never have more love or passion or commitment for Him than that which we understand He has for us. So as you boldly draw near to Jesus, enter into His presence and get to *know* Him in a much more intimate way, you will receive the revelation of His passion for you personally, the passionate love of the bridegroom for His bride. The Church is about to be swept off her feet. Instead of: *'My lover is mine and I am His.'* S of S 2:16 which is like the believer saying that they have invited Jesus into their life, but *they* are in control; it will be changed to: *'I am my lover's, and my lover is mine.'* S of S 6:3 – "I belong to Him, totally surrendered to *His* will. He is my Lord ."

Who is this King? ... I can talk about Him till the end of time, and I hope that you will see Him in my face and my life, but it is a question which you need to answer yourself. And the only way to do that is by drawing near to Him. You can read about Him in the Bible, and hear about Him through other people's testimony, but the only way to *know* Him is by revelation and guidance from the Holy Spirit as you come close to Him in relationship. Who is this King? … Do you *want* to know Him, *really* know Him? His love is given by grace, which is undeserved favour, to *anyone* who will reach out and receive it by faith. You cannot earn it but as you surrender and draw near to Him, realising that you are helpless without Him, He will surely draw near to you so that you *can* know Him. The Bible says,

> '*You will seek me and find me when you seek me with all your heart.*' Jer.29:13.

God is moving in the lives of His people throughout the whole world, setting them on fire with a passion for Him in a way that has never been known before. Who is this King? – He is The King of all Kings, Lord of lords, The Name above all names, Almighty God, creator of the Heavens and the earth and the rock on which I stand. He is my Lord, Redeemer, Saviour and Friend, Sovereign over every situation and circumstance. He is my Strength and Shield, the Rock on which I stand. The Bread of Life, the Veil that was torn and the East Gate giving entrance to the presence of God, Master, Teacher, Messiah. Healer. The Arm of the Lord, beloved Son of God, The Way, The Truth & The Life, the Wisdom of God, the Glory of God and The great I Am, Wonderful Counsellor, Mighty God Himself, Prince of Peace. He is the image of the invisible God, Emmanuel, The Light of the world, The Beginning and The End, Lamb of God and the Perfecter of my faith, my Shepherd and my Guide, The Holy one of Israel, The Word of God and the Answer to every question. He is the Breath of God and in fact The very reason that I live. He is my Joy, the Love of my life, He is Everything I could possibly need. He is my Husband and my lover … And I am married to Him for eternity … He is Jesus and I love Him!

The Plan of the Tabernacle

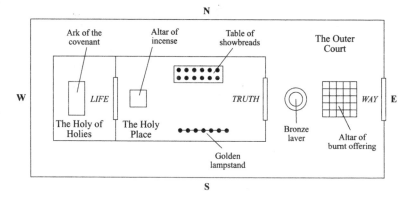

Further copies of this book
can be purchased by contacting:
Rose George, Advance International Ministries,
email: aim@gerry170.freeserve.co.uk

Website: www.aim170.org.co.uk

If you are a bookseller, no matter where you are in the world,
and you would like to sell this book to your customers,
please contact:

Harvest Fields Distribution
Unit 17 Churchill Business Park
Churchill Road
DONCASTER
DN1 2TF
UK

Tel: +44 (0)1302 367868
Fax: +44 (0)1302 361006
for wholesaling details.

**Obtaining your copies from these sources ensures that profits
from the sales go to extend God's Kingdom.**